How to Avoid Not Having
Enough Money To Live On
After Retirement

How to Avoid Not Having Enough Money To Live On After Retirement

Making Smarter and Simpler Decisions for Stress-free Retirement

Bob Kaye

WONDROUS WORDSMITHS
PUBLISHING

Los Angeles

ISBN: 978-1-7354226-0-2

Library of Congress Control Number: 2020913742

To the many people who wish to know what those money words mean,
but assume it will be too difficult to master
without a large amount of study.

Table of Contents

Introduction   11

Chapter One
Simple Investment Theory   15

Chapter Two
Media   19

Chapter Three
When to Put Money Where   21

Chapter Four
Places to Put Money   25

Chapter Five
Ways to Hold Money   29

Chapter Six
Making Money Grow — Stock   33

Chapter Seven
Making Money Grow — Bond   39

Chapter Eight
Making Money Grow — Mutual Fund   43

Chapter Nine
Making Money Grow — Mutual Fund Types   47

Chapter Ten
Making Money Grow — Mutual Fund Shares   53

Chapter Eleven
Making Money Grow — Mutual Fund Costs   55

Chapter Twelve
Making Money Grow — Fine Tuning   59

Chapter Thirteen
People Who Handle Money   65

Chapter Fourteen
How Did It Do?   69

Chapter Fifteen
Tax   77

Chapter Sixteen
Ways to Save Tax — Retirement Plans   81

Chapter Seventeen
Ways to Save Tax — Annuities   85

Chapter Eighteen
Ways to Save Tax — Annuities Features   89

Chapter Nineteen
Ways to Save Tax — Annuities Cost   93

Chapter Twenty
Protecting the Money and the Income — Life Insurance   95

Chapter Twenty-One
Protecting the Money and the Income — Cash Value Life Insurance 97

Chapter Twenty-Two
Protecting the Money and the Income — Life Insurance Guarantees 101

Chapter Twenty-Three
Switching the Money from One Place to Another   103

Chapter Twenty-Four
Taking Money Out   105

Chapter Twenty-Five
    Taking Money Out — Annuities   107

Chapter Twenty-Six
    Transferring Money at Death — Methods   109

Chapter Twenty-Seven
    Transferring Money at Death — to Whom?   111

Chapter Twenty-Eight
    Transferring Money at Death —
        Taxes and Fees   113

Chapter Twenty-Nine
    Transferring Money at Death —
        Saving Taxes and Fees   115

Conclusion   119
Next Steps   123
References   125
Crossword Puzzle Answer Key   127
About the Author   133

Introduction

Not having enough money to live on is a concern that has been voiced repeatedly by those getting closer to retirement. In working with such people for over 25 years, a common denominator arose which resolved much of this worry opening the door to planning for a retirement which is free from unnecessary stress and apprehension.

It has become more and more evident that such a resolution revolves around truly understanding the key individual words and terms connected and integral to the subject.

Welcome to the world of terminology.

In the following pages, I define terms in a simple way for the average consumer. The definitions are not meant for financial advisors, financial professionals, professors, economists, or anyone with advanced understanding of financial areas.

These terms are defined solely from my experience, which spans more than twenty-five years as an advisor in the financial industry. The definitions are not compilations of others' such definitions, so no references or sources are listed. What is written here is, in many cases, likely to go against currently held beliefs, terminology, definitions, and generally "known" data, as well as voluminous literature on the subject.

In my work with investors who are planning for retirement, I have found that there is generally a limited understanding of the simple terms that follow. This is the case even with those whose assets total in the millions of dollars, sometimes particularly so.

I have found in working with clients, families, business owners, and professionals that they are reluctant to advertise a lack of knowledge in such financial and investment areas because they may feel that they are the only ones who do not easily understand the details of investment theory, investment terminology, the myriad types of retirement plans, tax statuses, and so on. They are reluctant to admit they would prefer a grade school approach rather than a graduate school approach to these areas, when in fact, such an approach is exactly what is needed.

I have also found that there is considerable false information that is generally accepted to be true in the investment field. The most paramount examples of false data would, I believe, be those propounded by the media, specializing in information which is applicable for the minute and the hour but rarely for any long period of time, when in fact *long term* is the type of investment most persons planning for retirement are interested in. Instead, the public's attention is continually fixed on *short term* or *very short term* or *extremely short term,* and this is quite detrimental to their planning for the future, to say nothing of their nerves.

Further false information is contained in numerous published works concerning the subjects of money, investing, retirement planning, and how and when to invest correctly. You have only to review the many conflicting opinions, statements, and advice to recognize that much must be false, simply because there are so many whose opinions conflict with so many others in this area.

To make matters more confusing, the authors of such material appear to have extensive credentials, experience, footnotes, and references to support their view.

There are numerous well-written works on the subjects of investing, retirement planning, and finance as well. Some are more advanced than others, and unfortunately, some of the better texts are not written for the lay person who simply wants to understand a few things about their own retirement planning and does not intend to become an astute investor or expert in advanced planning.

If there is such a gap that could be filled with an easily understandable grade school primer, not written for children but for adults specifically, this is that book.

To be truly educational, the explanation of basic terminology is here outlined in a workbook fashion, with multiple crosswords to better allow you not only to browse or read over the material, but also to learn these basics fully in such a way that you can rely on as stable information for your financial planning.

The idea of *basics* cannot be accented enough. In any field, there are basics. Mastering the basics is key. Certainly, there are college graduates who have not mastered the basics of their field. These graduates may be outmaneuvered and left behind by someone with much less official education who has mastered the basics of only their field and nothing more, but in a relatively short time.

This book contains on the order of one hundred definitions of key terms which pertain to money, investing, and retirement planning. There are, of course, many more terms that could be included on this subject. Those included here should be the most needed to attain a basic understanding and an ability to work with such terms in this field.

The basics of a field must be correct. Unfortunately, in the field of finance, there are a very high number of theories, advices, methods, and more that are purported to be basics but are not. They are, in some cases, true but not of high importance and in other cases, outrightly false.

A fundamental test of any data is: can they be used?

I hope that you can indeed use the following information not only for better understanding of a field fraught with conflicting opinions, but most importantly, for better application to your own financial success.

CHAPTER ONE

Simple Investment Theory

To invest successfully over a lifetime does not require a stratospheric IQ, unusual business insights, or inside information.
What's needed is a sound intellectual framework for making decisions and the ability to keep emotions from eroding that framework.
~ Warren Buffet

The principle lesson of this book is that through time, the after-inflation returns on a well-diversified portfolio of common stocks have not only exceeded that of fixed income assets but have actually done so with less risk.
~ Jeremy Siegel

The bona fide investor does not lose money merely because the market price of his holdings declines; hence the fact that a decline may occur does not mean he is running a true risk of loss. If a group of well-selected common-stock investments shows a satisfactory overall return, as measured through a fair number of years, then this group investment has proved to be "safe."
~ Benjamin Graham

The great long-term, real-life financial risk isn't loss of principal, but erosion of purchasing power.
~ Nick Murray

Investment – this is defined by *Merriam-Webster's Dictionary* as an outlay of money for income or profit. The idea is to make some gain on the money. Please note that the definition itself does not propose any guarantee or even suggestion that you would get any of your money back. Per this definition, putting money under a mattress would not qualify as *investment*.

Word Origin

Investment is from the Latin, **vestis** clothing, garment. (You could say you're selecting the best wardrobe for retirement.)

Risk – this is generally considered to be the possibility of loss. But the definition usually does not include short-term or long-term loss, which it should. If the advice you receive is "the investment could go down, so it's risky," this logic may get you in trouble. A twenty-year investment in the stock market, which goes up and down but could increase eight times (close to historical average), might be less risky in the long term than a twenty-year investment in a savings account. This is because the savings account does not go down but may increase by only two times. The loss of the other potential six times the investment could have earned may be considerable. But a one-year investment in the stock market might be quite risky.

The Whole Story

What is *not* true about Risk:

Risk is not any investment that will fluctuate. Risk is not any investment in the stock market, no matter for how long or short.

Safety – this is generally considered to be insurance against loss. Again, this definition does not include short-term or long-term safety. The idea, "It doesn't go down, so it's safe," may not include all aspects of safety. A twenty-year investment in a savings account that doubles during that time may not be as "safe" as a twenty-year fluctuating market investment that might go up eight times in value (close to historical average).

The Whole Story

What is *not* true about Safety:

Safety is not lack of market volatility at any time.

Safety is not being "diversified" into short-term, "low-risk" investments used for long-term investment.

Safety is not *guaranteed* rates, whether they be high or low.

Inflation – this refers to inflating (increasing) the money supply, either by printing more money or by the extension of credit, which has the same effect. When the money supply is increased to cover the same amount of goods, this usually results in an increase in prices overall. Due to the fact that governments tend to keep increasing money supply to pay their bills, inflation tends to continue and can be a major factor to consider when doing any retirement planning or planning that involves spending funds at a future date. So, if inflation is at 3% and you make only 2% in a savings account, you can be losing money effectively in the long term, at an earnings rate of minus 1%.

Why Does Anyone Need Higher Returns: *INFLATION*

- The rule of 72 applies to inflation, in reverse.

- If inflation moves upward at 4%, then the cost of living will double every 18 years.

- In 36 years 1 million dollars will be worth only $250,000.

CHAPTER TWO

Media

The sillier the market's behavior, the greater the opportunity for the business-like investor. Follow Graham and you will profit from folly rather than participate in it.

~ Warren Buffet

But it is absurd to think that the general public can ever make money out of market forecasts.

~ Benjamin Graham

The worst course an investor can take is to follow the prevailing sentiment about economic activity. This will lead to buying at high prices when times are good and everyone is optimistic and selling at the low when the recession nears its trough and pessimism prevails.

~ Jeremy Siegel

Don't follow the crowd.

~ Philip Fisher

Soar – this is the media's sensationalist terminology for "go up."

Plummet – this is the media's sensationalist terminology for "go down."

Maybe I'll just take the stairs . .

News – it is ironic that we generally know that the news specializes in disaster, yet we are not particularly suspicious when we check the investment stock market news and it frequently turns out to be disaster.

Word Origin

News comes from "new"—the media feel that news must be "new" whereas the stock market has been the same old story for decades. They keep trying to insist that it is not the same old story.

CHAPTER THREE

When to Put Money Where

At the risk of being repetitious, let me underscore my belief that the short-term price movements are so inherently tricky to predict that I do not believe it possible to play the in–and-out game and still make the enormous profits that have accrued again and again to the truly long-term holder of the right stocks.

~ Philip Fisher

Not owning equities, especially during a thirty-year retirement, will prove fatal to wealth as we've defined it.

~ Nick Murray

Fear has a far greater grasp on human action than does the impressive weight of historical evidence.

~ Jeremy Siegel

Short-Term Investments – for example, are savings accounts and certificates of deposit. Usually any place to put money with a guaranteed rate is a short-term investment. This is because you do not usually want money to fluctuate in value if you need it soon.

The line of demarcation between what is considered *short term* and *long term* is about five years. This is because historically, in most cases, after five years, the market may be up or even, but not significantly down. This is not true of shorter periods such as two or three years.

The Whole Story

It is very, very, *very* important that you first understand the difference between short-term and long-term investment before investing. Failure to understand this simple distinction is responsible for quite a large degree of consumer upset with investments and their performance in general.

Important:
Long Term vs *Short* Term

- Due to the frequent ups and downs of stock investments, they are usually only a correct investment for the *long* term, 4 - 5 yrs. or more.

- If the time horizon is less than 4-5 yrs, then this is *short* term money and is best placed in savings or CDs or "fixed accounts".

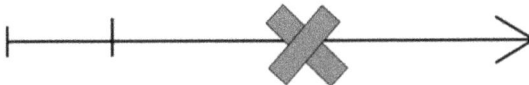

Long-Term Investments – usually investments in the stock market. They are long term because they are likely to fluctuate in value and therefore would not work well for money that might be needed just a few months or a year or two later.

Important: *Long* Term versus *Short* Term

Due to the frequent ups and downs of stock (and even bond) investments, they are usually only a correct investment for the *long* term, four to five years or more.

If the time horizon is less than four to five years, then this is *short*-term money and is best placed in savings, or CDs, or *fixed accounts*.

CHAPTER FOUR

Places to Put Money

Today, people who hold cash equivalents feel comfortable. They shouldn't. They have opted for a terrible long-term asset, one that pays virtually nothing and is certain to depreciate in value.

~ Warren Buffet

The only rational long-term definition of "money" is "purchasing power." And the real risk isn't losing your money. It's outliving it.

~ Nick Murray

Bank – a bank holds savings accounts and CDs, and both may increase in value. Banks now handle some stock market investments as well, whereas they did not originally do this.

Brokerage – comes from *broker*, which means either one who buys or sells for another or one who acts as an agent for another or a company. Therefore, *brokerage* is either:

1. A business that buys and sells for another, such as stocks, mutual funds, and so on. Specifically, a brokerage can buy and sell a large number of investments for another and thus save them time by going directly to individual mutual fund companies, for example, to buy a fund from that company. Some better-known financial brokerages are Morgan Stanley, Merrill Lynch, and Edward Jones.

2. A business that acts as an agent for another but in another capacity than investments. For example, a brokerage could shop for insurance companies to fit a particular client's needs and match the client with that insurance company, thereby acting as an agent for the client in his search for a good company.

Brokerage Account – an account at a brokerage in which you can hold individual mutual funds or stocks or bonds. It can be an IRA or non-tax sheltered. It is distinct from an *annuity*, which is not a brokerage account.

Fee-Based Account – a type of brokerage account in which there is one fee on the entire account, as compared with separate fees for each purchase.

Life Insurance Company – a company that provides life insurance or annuities. Annuities are also provided by life insurance companies due to the fact that annuities generally include certain insurance-like features such as guarantees against risk, lifetime payouts, and so on.

Mutual Fund Company – a company that handles and manages one single family of mutual funds. Examples are Fidelity, Putnam, and Franklin Templeton. This differs from a brokerage in that you have immediate access only to the funds in one fund family, whereas with a brokerage you may have access to a much broader array of funds crossing many mutual fund companies.

CHAPTER FIVE

Ways to Hold Money

A totally fixed-income strategy in a rising-cost world is suicide. It may be suicide on the installment plan, but it's still a plan for suicide.
~ Nick Murray

Fears regarding long-term prosperity of the nation's many sound companies make no sense. These businesses will inevitably suffer earnings hiccups, as they always have. But most major companies will be setting new profit records 5, 10, and 20 years from now.
~ Warren Buffet

The near complete failure of gold to protect against a loss in the purchasing power of the dollar must cast grave doubt on the ability of the ordinary investor to protect himself against inflation by putting his money in "things."
~ Benjamin Graham

Certificate of Deposit – like a savings account, but the money is committed for a certain period of time, such as six months or a year, and therefore earns a slightly higher interest rate.

Money Market – a relatively safer place to put funds for a short period of time. A money market earns a similar or slightly greater amount than a savings account.[1]

    A. This is the place where funds go when a fund is sold. If you hear that the funds are in the money market, it could mean that the sale is complete, as this is where the money automatically ends up. When dealing with a brokerage account, you cannot purchase new funds unless the funds are in the money market, so this is what you want to hear if you are going to purchase new funds. (This is not the case in an annuity, where one can switch or purchase or change funds anytime.)

    B. Someone could put funds into a money market directly as a sort of savings account. This is less common but could be done.

    C. Variable annuities do have a money market as one choice that clients could use, but you usually use the fixed account instead because it may pay a percentage or two higher interest. In addition, it usually has a minimum interest rate guarantee.

Securities (also referred to as *Stock Market,* or simply *the Market*) – refers to stocks, bonds, mutual funds, and some similar investments. It may seem strange that such investments are referred to as *securities* rather than "insecurities." The best reason that can be given for this is that these investments do have a

---

1 An investment in a money market is not insured or guaranteed by the Federal Deposit Insurance Corporation or any other government agency. Although a money market fund seeks to preserve the value of your investment at $1.00 per share, it is possible to lose money by investing in a money market fund.

certain security to them. That is, that you cannot lose more money than you invested. You generally cannot end up owing more money. Whereas, in a private business, you could invest a certain sum of money, lose all of it, and on top of that, end up legally owing more debts that the business incurred as well. Securities usually refer to investments in corporations that by law give the investors in the corporation more safety than investors in private businesses, which are not corporations.

Proprietary Investment – an investment product which is *proprietary* to a certain company. This means it can be held only at a certain company or brokerage and at no other. It denotes a situation where the investor is tied to a certain company at which investments may be held with no choice to easily move to another while holding the same investment.

Word Origin
Proprietary is related to the word "property," meaning that something is owned, exclusive to one owner.

Alternative Investment – an investment which is not in usual investments such as stocks, bonds, and mutual funds but in an investment vehicle which generally carries more risk and for which an investor may need to specially qualify in terms of assets or income or both. You may be tempted to invest in an Alternative Investment for some hope of higher return or benefit. It is important to understand that you may engage quite satisfactorily in general retirement planning without being involved in Alternative Investments. If you ask about an investment that is not included in these pages, it may likely be that it fits under Alternative Investment.

CHAPTER SIX

Making Money Grow — Stock

Stocks should constitute the overwhelming proportion of all long-term, financial portfolios. Based on historical evidence, even the most conservative investors should place most of their financial wealth in common stocks.

~ Jeremy Siegel

Listed on the various stock exchanges of the nation today are not just a few, but scores of companies in which it would have been possible to invest, say, $10,000 somewhere between twenty-five and fifty years ago and today have this purchase represent anywhere from $250,000 to several times this amount.

~ Philip Fisher

Over a ten-year period the typical excess of stock earning power over bond interest may aggregate 50% of the price paid.

~ Benjamin Graham

Stock (also referred to as ***Equities***) – shares of ownership in a large company. Companies sell shares of ownership to raise more money to operate and expand.[2]

Overview

- There are two ways that governments and large corporations get capital for expansion:

- 1) *Stocks* are a share of ownership in a company. Your value goes up and down with the value of the company.

- 2) *Bonds* are a loan from you to a government or large corporation.

Share – one unit of ownership of stock or a mutual fund.

Word Origin
One is "sharing" ownership with others and thus one unit is called a ***share***.

---

2 Stock values fluctuate in price so that the value of an investment can go up or down depending on market conditions. Stock prices may fluctuate due to stock market volatility and market cycles, as well as circumstances specific to a company.

Share Values – refers to the values of any share of stock or mutual fund. Oftentimes a statement will list share values and on mutual funds list them out to several decimal places. This is not necessarily the most important information. People tend to note the overall dollar value before noting the many decimal places of a share value in a mutual fund.

How Can You Insure Against Living Too Long?

- It is best to plan to *triple* your income during retirement, to combat inflation.

- Equities are *insurance against living too long* just as life insurance is insurance against the risk of not living long enough.

- In the stock market, the advance is permanent, the declines are temporary. The price of permanent advance is *full participation* in temporary declines.

Chapters One through Six

Across

2 Depends on the length of term

4 Insurance company

5 Increasing money supply

7 For savings accounts

8 Outlay of money for income or profit

10 Go down

13 A temporary holding place for

14 One unit of

15 Not critical to profitable investment

17 Go up

20 One overall fee

Down

1 Duration

3 Five years or less

4 Over five years

6 Manages one family only

7 A business which buys and sells for another

9 Only one company

11 Investments in corporations

12 That is not really new

16 Another word for stocks

18 Certificate of

19 Depends on long term or short term

WORD LIST

ALTERNATIVE	FUNDCOMPANY	NEWS	SHARE
BANK	INFLATION	PLUMMET	SHORT
BROKERAGE	INVESTMENT	PROPRIETARY	SOAR
DEPOSIT	LIFE	RISK	TERM
EQUITIES	LONG	SAFETY	
FEEBASED	MONEYMARKET	SECURITIES	

CHAPTER SEVEN

Making Money Grow — Bond

The investor should be aware that even though safety of its principal and interest may be unquestioned, a long-term bond could vary widely in market price in response to changes in interest rates.
~ Benjamin Graham

The real long-term total return of equities is so much greater than that of bonds that holding bonds is irrational for the true wealth seeker.
~ Nick Murray

Bond (also referred to as *Debt*) – a big word for loan. Means a loan from an individual to a corporation or a government. There are specific rules about amount and other stipulations.[3]

Word Origin
Bond is related to "bind" – one is bound to pay back the loan.

Interest – money paid in exchange for a loan, such as on a *bond* or savings account.

The Whole Story
Some people get "interest" mixed up with the "returns" on investments, such as stocks. Stocks do not earn interest but rather make a certain overall return composed of appreciation and dividends.

Short-Term Bond – this means that the "loan" needs to be paid back in from one to five years.

Long-Term Bond – this means that the "loan" needs to be paid back in a greater number of years, ranging up to as long as thirty years.

Municipal Bond, Muni – also referred to as *Tax-Free Bond* - a bond in which an investor "loans" money to a municipality, a city. These bonds are usually income tax free on the interest that is paid by the city to the bondholder, so become popular for this reason, although they likely pay a lower rate of interest due to this factor.[4]

---

3 Bonds are subject to interest rate risk. Bond prices generally fall when interest rates rise.
4 Municipal bonds may subject investors to the Alternative Minimum Tax (AMT). Municipal bonds are usually exempt from state and local taxes, though discount bonds may be subject to capital gains tax.

The Whole Story

Tax-free bonds are more likely appropriate for persons with very high incomes but are often illogically found in the portfolios of persons with very low incomes.

A tax-free bond is tax free on the interest but not tax free on the gain or loss in the value of the bond. So, if the bond is sold before its maturity, there may be a gain or loss compared to the purchase price. This gain will not be tax free but will be what is called a *capital gain*.

CHAPTER EIGHT

Making Money Grow — Mutual Fund

We are quite certain that the funds in the aggregate have served a useful purpose. They have promoted good habits of savings and investment; they have protected countless individuals against costly mistakes in the stock market; they have brought their participants income and profits commensurate with the overall returns from common stocks.

~ Benjamin Graham

Although it might appear to be riskier to hold stocks than bonds, precisely the opposite is true: the safest long-term investment for the preservation of purchasing power has clearly been stocks, not bonds.

~ Jeremy Siegel

Over the long term, the stock market news will be good. In the 20th century, the United States endured two world wars and other traumatic and expensive military conflicts; the Depression; a dozen or so recessions and financial panics; oil shocks; a flu epidemic; and the resignation of a disgraced president. Yet the Dow rose from 66 to 11,497.

~ Warren Buffet

The Solution To Individual Stock Volitility

- Stocks alone can soar or drop to very low values, much more so than the average market. To effect average market returns with average voliltility compared to individual stocks, the *mutual fund* was born.

- A mutual fund allows an investor to invest in *about 100 stocks at one time* conveniently and easily and thereby expect average returns of all of those stocks put together.

The Whole Story

Some people get mutual funds and individual stocks mixed up, as in, "How are my stocks doing?" when they own mutual funds. As the risk can be significantly different, it is important to keep these differentiated.

Mutual Fund – an arrangement in which someone buys about a hundred different stocks (or bonds or combination of stocks and bonds) all at one time but which requires only a minimum investment. It is usually a much safer way to invest than buying only one or two stocks. Mutual funds have become more popular in the last few decades, during which time their numbers have greatly increased.

There are two ways that large corporations and governments obtain capital to operate. These are called *stocks* and *bonds*. Stocks are a share of ownership in a company. Bonds are simply a loan, but on a corporate or government scale.

As you probably know, dealing with stocks by themselves can be kind of risky. You own a share of the company and if the company goes under and is worth nothing, your share is worth nothing—you can lose all your investment. Some time ago, someone came up with the idea of putting a whole bunch of stocks together into one investment. This is what is called a *mutual fund*. There are usually something like a hundred different companies that you are investing in at the same time this way. This greatly diversifies your investment and is generally much safer. Even if one of the companies—and these are large companies—even if one of them went completely under, you might barely notice the difference in your overall investment. Each company could be only 1 or 2% of your total investment.

Mutual Fund Family – mutual funds come in groups all under the same overall company which sponsors a certain number of individual funds. There may be anywhere from a few funds in one family to a hundred different funds. Some better-known fund family names are Fidelity, Oppenheimer, Kemper, American, Delaware, Janus, Putnam, and Franklin Templeton.

Equity Funds and *Bond Funds* – equity refers to the fact that the investment is in stocks as opposed to bonds or vice versa. Stocks may be referred to generally as *equities* whereas bonds may be referred to generally as *debt*.

Prospectus – a full disclosure of all the information about a mutual fund. It is required by law that it be given to the investor. It is usually a booklet with a considerable amount of small print, up to one hundred pages long. If an investor is given any material about a fund, this must be included. ***Mutual funds are sold by prospectus only. Investors should read the prospectus carefully before investing and consider objectives, risks, charges, and expenses of the fund carefully. The fund prospectus contains this and other important information. For a copy of the prospectus contact your financial advisor.***

Word Origin

Prospectus is from the Latin *spectare,* to see and *pro,* before.

CHAPTER NINE

Making Money Grow — Mutual Fund Types

Only those who will be sellers of equities in the near future should be happy at seeing stocks rise. Prospective purchasers should much prefer sinking prices.

~ Warren Buffet

There should be adequate, though not excessive, diversification.

~ Benjamin Graham

It is irrational in the extreme for someone who is not finished buying yet to want the market to go up.

~ Nick Murray

Large Cap, Medium Cap, and *Small Cap* – Stocks, and by logical extension mutual funds, are divided into three basic categories: small, medium, and large. The size is determined by the total stock value at any one time—in other words, what the entire company would sell for if one person were to purchase all the stock at one time. This is also referred to as *market capitalization* or *market cap.* The approximate size categories are as follows, but these categories are themselves gradually changing through time as businesses keep expanding.

Small: approximately 300 million to 2 billion dollars.[5]

Medium: approximately 2 billion to 10 billion dollars.[6]

Large: approximately 10 billion dollars and up.

---

5 Small-capitalization investing typically carries more risk than investing in well-established "blue-chip" companies, since smaller companies generally have a higher risk of failure. Historically, smaller companies' stock has experienced a greater degree of market volatility than the average stock.

6 Mid-capitalization investing typically carries more risk than investing in well-established "blue-chip" companies. Historically, mid-cap companies' stock has experienced a greater degree of market volatility than the average stock.

Small, Medium and Large

- Like the coffees at Starbucks, stocks come in small medium and large.

- *Small* is from about 300 million to about 2 billion dollars total value of the company: Papa John's Pizza, etc.

- Medium is around 2 to 10 billion value: Nordstrom, etc.

- Large is over about 10 billion value: Microsoft, Disney, etc.

Value – Another separate categorization to apply to mutual funds/stocks one holds is the distinction between *growth* and *value* stocks. Value means a stock's price has for some reason dropped significantly and can now be purchased at a bargain, providing the reason is not a particularly long-term one.

One can crisscross small, medium, and large with growth and value and come up with a sort of grid to put any mutual fund on.

Value	Growth	
		Large
		Medium
		Small

Growth – Growth means a stock price is growing steadily and may continue to do so and therefore, may be considered a good investment, depending on one's investment goals and objectives.

The Two Investing Strategies: Value and Growth

- The manager of a mutual fund who buys stocks at a bargain and waits for them to increase in value is said to be managing a "value" fund.

- The manager who buys stocks which are steadily increasing in value is said to be managing a "Growth" fund.

- Neither of these to strategies may be superior, but rather complement each other.

The Cyclic Nature of Equity Investment Classes

- Small and Large, as well as Value and Growth do not usually all move up and down at the same time but rather at random or opposite times.

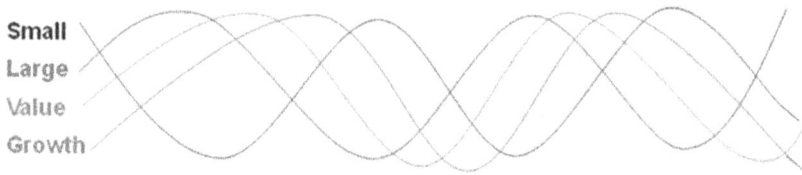

Small
Large
Value
Growth

- The average may be a much smoother ride

CHAPTER TEN

Making Money Grow —
Mutual Fund Shares

It is vastly more difficult to predict what a particular stock
is going to do in the next six months.

~ Philip Fisher

A Shares – mutual funds are divided into three (or sometimes more) types of shares. "A" shares often have a sales charge of about 6% that the investor must pay up front.

The Whole Story

Often when looking on a statement for an investment account, you may see mutual funds listed. Part of the name of the fund will be the Share Class. For example: Best Investment Fund A, or Best Investment Fund B.

B Shares – have a "contingent deferred sales charge" which means the charge starts at, say, 6% but goes down each year to zero over about five years, so if you withdraw funds after five years there is no charge.

C Shares – have no immediate charge but cost a bit more in expense charges. If sold within one year only, there may be a 1% charge.

The Whole Story

When you sell and then buy a new fund within the same family there may be no charge to do so.

CHAPTER ELEVEN

Making Money Grow — Mutual Fund Costs

The market may ignore business success for a while,
but eventually will confirm it.

~ Warren Buffet

Expense Charge – refers to the expenses of managing the fund itself. These can range from less than 1% up to 2% or more.

The Whole Story

With the same return expected, of course lower expense charges would be preferable to higher expense charges. It is important to understand, however, that one would be better off with a fund with a 12% return and a 2% expense charge netting 10% return than one would with a fund with a 10% return and a 1% expense charge netting 9% return—half the expense charge but still 1% less return overall.

Load – refers to a sales charge on a mutual fund. A load fund means a fund which has a sales charge, A, B, or C share. The majority of mutual funds are load funds.

No Load – refers to a mutual fund without a sales charge. Some people get the idea that this is better and cheaper and that they should only buy no-load funds. They forget about the fund management expense which can vary widely and sometimes be more than a sales charge plus management expense charge on another fund. No load also means no advice. The investor is completely on their own.

Load Waived – Under a special arrangement, both load and no-load funds can be used in *fee-based accounts* in which the load is waived on the load funds on initial purchase, but a fee is charged on the entire account overall. Such an arrangement gives the individual investor access to all or many funds, whether load or no load, on an equal charge basis.

Chapters Seven through Eleven

Across

1 A big word for loan

4 7 billion

6 Tax free

8 Bargain

11 Disclosure

13 Contingent charge

14 Means shared

15 For fee-based

17 GE

19 Increasing

Down

2 No sales charge

3 800 million

5 Fund management

7 Earned on bonds not stocks

9 No immediate charge

10 Sales charge

12 Group of funds

16 Simpler word for bond

18 Mutual fund sales charge

WORD LIST

ASHARE	EXPENSE	LOAD	PROSPECTUS
BOND	FAMILY	MEDIUM	SMALL
BSHARE	GROWTH	MUNI	VALUE
CSHARE	INTEREST	MUTUAL	WAIVED
DEBT	LARGE	NOLOAD	

CHAPTER TWELVE

Making Money Grow — Fine Tuning

Don't overstress diversification.

~ Philip Fisher

The third is the device of "dollar cost averaging," which means simply that the practitioner invests in common stocks the same number of dollars each month or each quarter. In this way, he buys more shares when the market is low than when it is high, and he is likely to end up with a satisfactory overall price for all his holdings.

~ Benjamin Graham

Dollar Cost Averaging empowers you to experience bear markets as an opportunity rather than a victim.

~ Nick Murray

Trading – refers to a transaction wherein a stock or mutual fund is bought or sold.

Diversification – means investing in more than one area so that if one goes down, the other may go up, and one may achieve a smoother ride overall.[7]

Diversification: A Scale

- Not diversified: few stocks or bonds in same asset class

- Barely diversified: 10-20 Stocks
                              10-20 bonds

- Poorly diversified: 1 mutual fund
                           = 100 stocks or bonds
                              in one asset class

- Well diversified: Several mutual funds in different asset classes
  3-400 stocks or bonds

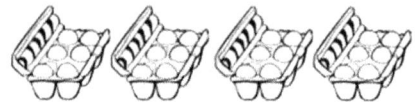

---

7 Diversification does not guarantee a profit or protection from losses in a declining market.

The Whole Story

It is important in attempting to diversify that you pay attention to the asset classes into which you are diversifying. The best example of diversification is a mutual fund. As opposed to owning one stock, which may fluctuate greatly in value and could even lose all its value, you instead own something like a hundred similar category stocks and achieve greater relative safety thereby. An example of less-than-effective—even damaging—diversification would be diversifying to include bonds with stocks in a portfolio, or bond funds with stock funds. This is due to the fact that bonds generally experience a significantly lower long-term return than equities (stocks). You would be lowering your overall average return in so doing. Much better would be to simply allocate short-term investments to bonds, or less fluctuating assets, and long-term investments to equities. In this way, long-term investing would not be compromised.

Rebalancing or *Fund Rebalancing* – the action of periodically rebalancing the percentages of mutual funds in a portfolio to their original allocations. As one fund does better and another does worse, the allocation will become unbalanced from the original. Rebalancing automatically sells high and buys low, which is a positive way to earn more income on investments, providing that they are all invested in equities. If you rebalance periodically but one of the allocations is a bond fund, then this will result in continually adding some earnings of the equity funds to the bond fund over long periods, not necessarily likely to increase overall performance.

The Whole Story

General fund rebalancing is often mixed up with *equity rebalancing*. The two can have opposite effects. When rebalancing includes bonds or bond funds, the rebalancing will sell equities (stocks) and put the proceeds into bonds. While increasing the relative percentage of bonds in the account, this action will not increase overall return but will more likely decrease it. When rebalancing an account that includes equities only, such rebalancing will likely increase overall returns as one is selling high and buying low on a periodic basis which will likely increase overall returns of the account.

Quite often, any form of rebalancing is left out altogether. This is not preferred as it can be costly. One should check in any investment to see whether there is fund rebalancing occurring or not.

Dollar Cost Averaging – refers to the action of putting money into an investment by the month, rather than all at once. This has certain advantages and may cause a higher rate of return, since sometimes stocks are being purchased when prices are lower and more shares can be bought.

This happens automatically in many retirement accounts, most commonly when you make regular deposits from your paycheck into an account on a periodic basis. In such a case, to take advantage of dollar cost averaging, you would want to make sure that the funds being deposited to the account periodically were being deposited into equities, which fluctuate in value, as opposed to bonds or other less fluctuating investments.[8]

The Whole Story
Some people refer to *Dollar Cost Averaging* loosely as anytime investments are made periodically. This is incorrect. Dollar Cost Averaging is putting money into equities by the month. One hopes for the greatest fluctuation possible to realize the greatest return in dollar cost averaging. The lower the fluctuation, the less effective Dollar Cost Averaging will generally be.

---

8 Dollar cost averaging does not assure a profit and does not protect against loss in declining markets.

Allocation – refers to an account which contains several mutual funds. There can be percentages of each fund to make up the whole, such as: first fund, 30%; second fund, 40%; and third fund, 30%. Allocation is related to diversification, and if you are allocated in various parts of the market, this would contribute to diversification, assuming you are in all long-term investments or all short-term investments.

The Whole Story

The best example of misallocation is when an investor claims to be diversified and has five different funds total, but every one of them is in the same category—for example, large growth. This means that their five different funds are likely invested in nearly identical stocks.

CHAPTER THIRTEEN

People Who Handle Money

Try not to worry. Your advisor is doing that for you.
~ Nick Murray

For many investors, it is helpful to have an advisor who can lend a steady hand and maintain a proper long-term perspective for a portfolio.
~ Jeremy Siegel

If we assume that there are normal or standard income results to be obtained from investing money in securities, then the role of the advisor can be more readily established. He will use his superior training and experience to protect his clients against mistakes and to make sure that they obtain the results to which their money is entitled.
~ Benjamin Graham

Wealth Manager, also known as *Financial Advisor, Financial Planner* – a person who gives financial advice and usually has access to and provides various financial products for an investor.

The Whole Story

The idea of having a financial advisor has become a debatable subject. The opposite, of course, is Do It Yourself. In many areas of life, Do It Yourself can work. On the other hand, we've all had experiences where we wish we *hadn't* done it ourselves. One of the most important roles that a financial advisor can play is handling the emotions connected with market upturns and downturns. In other areas, with advances in technology, you can maybe select products on the internet and possibly invest. Handling emotions is the least likely, and most difficult, aspect of financial advice to replace. All the media focus you on thinking of the short term only. A good Financial Advisor will be useful in continually reminding you to think of the long term.

Registered Representative – one licensed to deal with securities investments, including mutual funds, with a generally broader view than a stockbroker, and not necessarily dealing with life insurance or broader planning.

Stockbroker – an advisor who specializes in and is licensed for buying and selling of stocks or bonds only for an investor.

Banker – one who specializes in banking and bank accounts.

Insurance Agent – one who specializes in and is licensed for insurance and annuities.

Independent Financial Advisor – an advisor who is free to represent and provide most all investments needed for a client without restriction and is not required to provide any proprietary products promoted by their sponsor company or broker dealer.

Independent Broker Dealer – a broker dealer is an organization which sponsors and handles supervision of Financial Advisors so that they may direct attention to servicing clients. An Independent Broker Dealer is a broker dealer that allows associated advisors to deal with most any financial product of their choosing to best fit the needs of the clients they are servicing.

Captive Financial Advisor – you will never hear this term used by an advisor, even if this is the true type of advice they give. It means that the advisor works for and is beholden to one company only and must provide only their products or mainly their products. This is not in the best interest of the consumer, as you may never hear about a wide range of investment products because the advisor is not allowed to deal with such products.

Comprehensive Financial Planning – financial advice or planning which covers all areas of concern for an individual, family, or business. This would include securities investment, life insurance and annuities, and estate planning. This would be best done by an Independent Financial Advisor.

The Whole Story

Dealing with only an insurance agent, or only a stockbroker, as opposed to a financial advisor who provides comprehensive financial planning can result in a lopsided portfolio accented towards the products that the particular agent is licensed to deal with.

The Whole Story

Unbeknownst to many consumers and investors, there are different licenses required to give different aspects of financial advice and to provide different financial products. It is preferable to deal with an advisor who has all the required licenses and so is better enabled to give impartial advice.

CHAPTER FOURTEEN

How Did It Do?

I have come to believe that the most that can be said on the subject of dividends is that it is an influence that should be downgraded very sharply by those that do not need the income.

~ Philip Fisher

Wealth isn't primarily determined by investment performance, but by investor behavior.

~ Nick Murray

For years, the financial services have been making stock market forecasts without anyone taking this activity very seriously. Like everyone else in the field, they are sometimes right and sometimes wrong.

~ Benjamin Graham

Dividend – earnings or profit from a company paid out to stockholders. Smaller growing companies usually do not pay dividends at all. Larger established companies usually pay dividends. Dividends from funds in retirement accounts are usually reinvested and not paid out directly to the account holder.[9]

The Whole Story

In times gone by, there has been considerable importance attached to dividends—this does not necessarily hold true today. When, in times before the popularity of mutual funds, you held stocks only, you could live on dividends from those stocks without selling shares of the stocks themselves. This also may have been before the invention and popularity of retirement accounts, such as IRAs. You could conceivably live off dividends today, but in the majority of cases, you would have a retirement account, and it would not matter if you received dividends or simply sold part of the stocks or the mutual funds as all distributions from the account—no matter what type—would be taxable. In an IRA made up of mutual funds, it is largely irrelevant whether your earnings are in the form of dividends or simply appreciation of the values of the shares.

Appreciation – Increase in value of a company, as opposed to payment of dividends. Together, appreciation and dividends make up the total return of a stock or mutual fund.

---

9 Dividend yield investing may not be suitable for all investors. You should never invest solely on the basis of dividends. Higher dividends are not indicative of the quality of an investment. Additionally, higher dividends will result in lower retained earnings. As dividend yields may not be sustainable, income investors must be sure to analyze an investment carefully along with their ability to sustain market fluctuations. Investments paying dividends do not carry lower risk. Dividend payments are not guaranteed by the issuing entity. The issuer can discontinue the dividend at any time. Dividend payments reduce the price of the security by the amount of the paid dividend.

Return, also referred to as ***Performance*** – the name for "interest rate" on a mutual fund. It changes so much that averages over longer periods of time are used. Actually, return on either a stock or a mutual fund is made up of two things:

The direct earnings, called *dividends* for stocks and *interest* for bonds.

The *appreciation,* or change in value over time.

Dividends, or interest, are paid out to the stock or bondholder periodically if they wish, or reinvested if they so direct. Appreciation may only be realized by selling the investment. Generally, on stocks or mutual funds holding stocks, the appreciation is the more important factor as it is usually much greater than dividends.

Morningstar – name of a company and computer program or application that deals with mutual funds directly, completes data about, and provides charting of returns over periods of time.

Rule of 72 – If you divide an interest rate into 72, the answer tells you how many years it will take for the sum of money to double, and vice versa. You may see how this works using a particular sum of money.[10]

For example, you have $30,000 in an investment making 6% interest now.

You are forty-one years old and plan to retire at age sixty-five, twenty-four years from now.

Dividing 72 by 6 (if return was 6%), your account value will double every twelve years, or twice before retirement.

_____

10 The Rule of 72 does not guarantee investment results or function as a predictor of how your investment will perform. It is simply an approximation of the impact a targeted rate of return would have. Investments are subject to fluctuating returns and there can never be a guarantee that any investment will double in value.

$30,000 doubled twice is $120,000.

Monthly interest-only payout on $120,000 is $120,000 x 6%, or $7,200.

$7,200 ÷ 12 months = $600 per month.

Now, compare a higher rate of return, such as 12%.

Dividing 72 by 12, your account value will double *every six years,* or *four times before retirement.*

$30,000 doubled 4 times is $480,000.

Monthly interest-only payout on $480,000 is 480,000 x 12% = $57,600. $57,600 ÷ 12 = $4,800 per month.

In this case, your monthly retirement goes up *from $600 per month to $4,800 per month, eight times,* as a result of increasing your account return to double the rate of return. The previous is purely theoretical, not based on any actual investment, but provides an idea how this can work.

"Guaranteed" – refers to an investment or feature of an investment that will not change in some manner or will not go below some stated rate.

Index – is an average return of a particular category of investment.[11]

There is such a thing as an **Index Fund,** which invests in an index only. Such funds have gained some popularity. They do provide the security that one will not do much worse than the index, as they do have expense fees. On the other hand, they also will virtually guarantee that you won't do better than the index, as they *are* the index.

---

11 An investor cannot invest directly in an index.

There is a further variation of an Index Fund, known as an ***Exchange Traded Fund*** or ***ETF***. Such a fund is usually an Index Fund but trades like a stock rather than a mutual fund; meaning, for example, that the price can fluctuate during the day as opposed to being fixed only at the end of the day as with a mutual fund.

Dow – is short for Dow Jones Industrial Average, the most famous and well-known group of stocks which represent an average of the stock market. It is a group of thirty large companies to which market returns are compared. As they are large companies, the Dow, in truth, is more like an index for large-sized companies only and should not usually be compared to small- or mid-sized companies; they have their own indexes for comparison.

The Whole Story
It is vital to know about indexes and which index will be comparable to your particular investment. For example, the S & P 500 is an index of 500 large-sized stocks. If you are investing in large-sized stocks, then you can compare your returns to this index to see how they are doing, whether ahead or behind.

Chapters Twelve through Fourteen

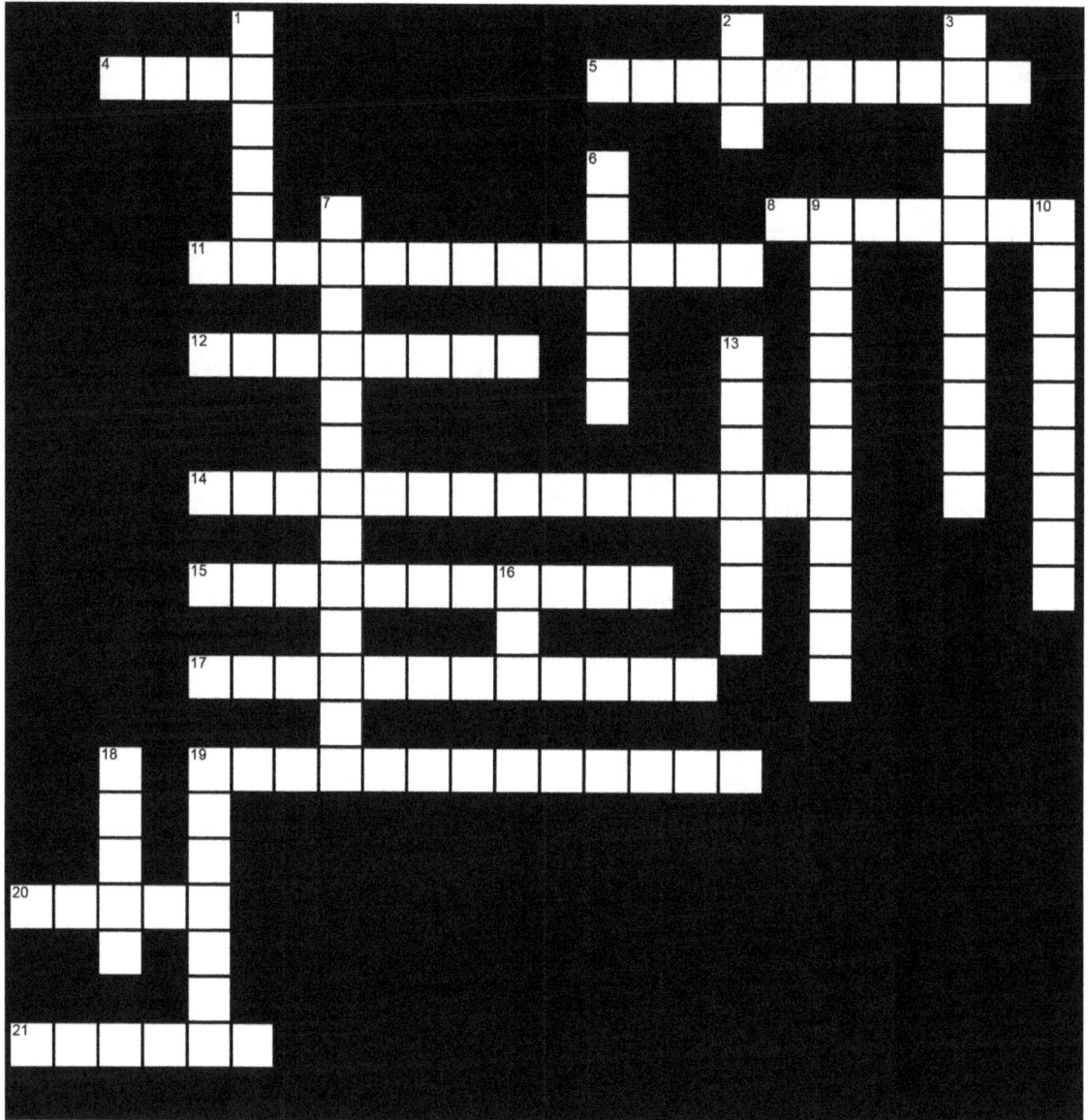

Across

4 Of 72

5 Correct diversificaon

8 Buying or selling

11 Widest product selection

12 Earnings paid

14 More than one place

15 Not proprietary

17 Increase in value

19 Covers all areas

20 Life and annuities

21 Sells stocks and bonds

Down

1 Same as performance

2 Average of market

3 Full mutual fund data

6 Accounts

7 General investments

9 Sells high, buys low

10 Will not change

13 Financial advice

16 Better into equities

18 Return of a category

19 Beholden to one

WORD LIST

ADVISOR	COMPREHENSIVE	INDEPENDENTBD	TRADING
AGENT	DCA	INDEX	
ALLOCATION	DIVERSIFICATION	MORNINGSTAR	
APPRECIATION	DIVIDEND	REBALANCING	
BANKER	DOW	REGISTEREDREP	
BROKER	GUARANTEE	RETURN	
CAPTIVE	INDEPENDENT	RULE	

CHAPTER FIFTEEN

Tax

So, smile when you read a headline that says, "Investors lose as market falls." Edit it in your mind to "Disinvestors lose as market falls—but investors gain."

~ Warren Buffet

Doing what everybody else is doing at the moment, and therefore what you have an almost irresistible urge to do, is often the wrong thing to do at all.

~ Philip Fisher

Tax-law is subject to frequent change; therefore, it is important to coordinate with your tax advisor for the latest IRS rulings and specific tax advice, prior to undertaking an investment plan. Any tax or legal information provided here is merely a summary of and interpretation of some of the current income tax regulations.

Income Tax – tax in the United States that is levied on personal income either by Federal or State government. It is paid on personal earnings from employment, and additionally, it is paid on earnings from investments.

Internal Revenue Code or ***IRC*** – the code assigned by the IRS to various retirement plans. Many are named after the specific IRC, such as 401(k) and 403(b). Both these retirement plans refer to the section of the Internal Revenue Code which outlines their rules. The letter after the number ("k" or "b") refers to the subsection under the Internal Revenue Code number.

"Stock Tax" – while "stock tax" is not a term you will hear, it is important to differentiate what is the tax on individual stocks, as compared to other investments, particularly mutual funds, when they are not held as part of a tax-sheltered investment, such as an IRA. The main tax on a stock sale is likely to be *capital gains tax*. This will be realized all at once, when the stock shares are sold. The sale will be at the choice of the investor. You may be reluctant to make such a sale if there is significant gain, knowing that the gain will be realized and taxes will be due.

Mutual Fund Tax – the tax on a mutual fund is considerably different than that due on an individual stock sale. As a mutual fund is a managed basket of stocks, the sale of the stocks is not up to the investor but up to the mutual fund manager. Such sales happen all year long. Quite likely most or all the stocks have been sold during the year, and the greater part of the gain may be realized that year, not at the choice of the investor but regardless of their choice. In a non-tax-sheltered investment, such tax possibility will be important to consider as taxes need to be paid each year. In a tax-sheltered investment, there will likely be no tax paid until withdrawal at some point in the future so the significance of such gains will be little.

Tax Deferral – means that taxes are due but need not be paid until a later date, usually when funds are withdrawn. An IRA or 401(k) could be considered a tax-deferred investment as taxes will be due in the future when funds are withdrawn for use.

The Whole Story

The difference between tax-sheltered and non-tax-sheltered investment is important to understand. A tax-sheltered investment can appear carefree for years until such time as withdrawal may be required. A non-tax-sheltered investment may appear to be the opposite, fraught with worry about what will be the tax liability at the end of the year.

The Whole Story

Tax-sheltered investments, when they are taxed, usually upon withdrawal, are generally taxed at ordinary income tax rates. Non-tax-sheltered investments are normally taxed at capital gains rates, which in many or most cases are less than ordinary income tax rates. Does this mean that it is always better to have a non-tax-sheltered investment? The answer to this is that the tax-sheltered investment is in fact tax-sheltered and thereby, greatly delays the payment of tax, allowing funds to gain earnings without taxes due for some time into the future. In many cases, this advantage may outweigh the seeming disadvantage of paying ordinary income taxes instead of capital gains taxes.

CHAPTER SIXTEEN

Ways to Save Tax — Retirement Plans

When all the factors are considered, it is better for most investors to hold stocks in their tax-deferred account rather than in their taxable account.
~ Jeremy Siegel

It is clear that those with a fixed dollar income will suffer when the cost of living advances.
~ Benjamin Graham

Individual Retirement Account or ***IRA*** – a retirement account that anyone may use to keep about $6,000 to $7,000 of their income per year (adjusted annually for inflation) from being taxed. Also, an account (could be the same one) into which someone can "rollover" funds from a 401(k) after they retire. IRAs are a form of account to be used for retirement only. As such, there is usually a 10% tax penalty if money is withdrawn before age fifty-nine-and-a-half and an up to 25% penalty on any money that is supposed to be withdrawn after age seventy-three.

Roth IRA – a newer IRA invented some years ago, sort of the opposite of a regular IRA. Instead of the money being tax deferred as it goes in and taxable when it comes out, a Roth IRA allows for already-taxed deposits, but when withdrawn, the money is not taxed again. You pay all the taxes up front instead of later. It was invented by Congressman Bill Roth. The rest of Congress thought it was such a good idea to convince people to want to pay taxes right away, they named it after him. Usually, it makes more sense to invest in a regular IRA, as it will save taxes now. A good reason to do a Roth IRA could be that 1) you have hardly any taxes now and have a low salary or are not working; 2) you are already maxed on regular pension plans such as 401(k)s or 403(b)s; or 3) you are converting a regular IRA or tax-sheltered account into a Roth IRA so it won't be taxed in the future.

401(k) – the IRS code number for retirement plans for profit companies as opposed to nonprofit which are more likely to use 403(b) plans. A 401(k) permits investments through only one company, as compared with 403(b)s, in which each person has choice of quite a number of companies to invest through. Also, it is not possible to transfer out of a 401(k) until the employee is terminated from service for the particular company they were working for which offered the 401(k), whereas in the case of 403(b), employees may transfer out at any time to other available investment choices.

Tax Sheltered Annuity, TSA, also ***403(b)*** – a special kind of annuity for teachers and employees of nonprofit companies only. The money they put in is taken out of their paycheck every month and there are certain limitations on how much they can put in. A 403(b) can also be invested in a custodial account that is not an annuity, in which case it is technically called a *403(b)(7) account.*

Please refer to irs.gov for further information on rules and contribution limits.

CHAPTER SEVENTEEN

Ways to Save Tax — Annuities

*The deferral of taxes on capital gains and dividends is usually worth
more than the advantage of the lower capital gains tax
in the taxable account.*

~ Jeremy Siegel

*The investor with a portfolio of sound stocks should expect their prices to
fluctuate and should neither be concerned by sizable declines nor become
excited by sizable advances. He should always remember that market
quotations are there for his convenience,
either to be taken advantage of or to be ignored.*

~ Benjamin Graham

*If you stay with the right stocks through even a major temporary market
drop, you are, at most, going to be temporarily behind 40% of the former
peak at the very worst point and will ultimately be ahead;
whereas if you sell* and don't buy back *you will have missed long-term
profits many times the short-term gains from having sold the stock in
anticipation at a short-term reversal.*

~ Philip Fisher

Annuity

1. *Regular and historical definition.* Originally meant a yearly payout of a sum of money as opposed to the recipient receiving it all at once. The *yearly* was then expanded to monthly, quarterly, and so on. This definition goes back in history hundreds of years. Originally, a number of people could all deposit money into one place, and then as each one died, the rest could be split between the others so that the final person living still had enough to last them for the rest of their life. This was a special idea so no one would run out of money, instead of each person being totally on their own.

2. *IRS definition.* Annuities have grown on a tax-deferred basis since enactment of the Federal Income Tax Code in 1913. Since they were issued by insurance companies, annuities were always able to accumulate without taxes being taken out at year-end. Additional rules were added, such as certain IRS rules about eventual withdrawal: you can't withdraw before age fifty-nine-and-a-half.

3. *Insurance Company definition.* The funds are now usually deposited with an insurance company and can go into either a *fixed annuity* or *variable annuity*. It is important to understand this definition separately from definition number 2 because sometimes funds are put into an annuity where the primary purpose of the annuity is not tax deferral. This can be in the case of an IRA or 403(b) being put into an annuity. In these cases, the funds already are tax deferred because they are in an IRA or 403(b). In this case, the annuity acts as another investment account with certain features that may not be available in a regular brokerage account for the same funds, such as:

1. Switching from one fund to another without new sales charge

2. *Automatic fund rebalancing* – not usually available on regular mutual fund accounts

3. *Death benefit guarantee* – a guarantee that the beneficiary will receive at least as much as was originally deposited into the annuity

4. *Guaranteed income benefit* – a guarantee that one will receive at least a certain amount of regular withdrawal regardless of the balance in the account

5. Possibly lower minimum balance to start the account

6. Arrangement for periodic payments to go into the account out of paychecks, a feature not available on all mutual fund accounts. Regulatory bodies give extra attention to IRAs, 403(b)s, and others going into annuities because sometimes the annuities have higher fees, so they check to ensure that there is a distinct benefit that you will receive directly from being in the annuity before letting you so invest.

Annuities are long-term investments designed for retirement purposes. Withdrawals of taxable amounts are subject to income tax and, if taken prior to age fifty-nine and a half, a 10% federal tax penalty may apply. Early withdrawals may be subject to withdrawal charges. Optional riders have limitations and are available for an additional cost through the purchase of a variable annuity contract. Guarantees are based on the claims-paying ability of the issuing company.

Fixed Annuity – an annuity in which all the money is guaranteed not to be lost and a certain interest rate is guaranteed for some period. In the long term, it may earn around half or less compared to a variable annuity.

Variable Annuity – an annuity which is invested in mutual funds. It was first originated in 1952. Nothing is guaranteed. It also may include within it a *fixed account*, which is like having a fixed annuity within the variable annuity. The account holder does not have to put any funds into the fixed annuity portion but may if they wish in order to have more security on some of the funds.

Index Annuity, also ***Equity Index Annuity, EIA*** – a type of fixed annuity invented around the turn of the century and becoming popular only in the last twenty years or so. It attempts to connect in some way to the stock market, thereby giving investors the usually misunderstood idea that they are in the stock market but without any risk. In fact, the interest credited in an equity index annuity is similar to that in a fixed annuity, a bit higher when interest rates are down, but not equally comparable to real, long-term stock market returns realized in a variable annuity. An equity index annuity also usually has high surrender charges and complicated provisions describing how interest is credited.

CHAPTER EIGHTEEN

Ways to Save Tax — Annuities Features

Let me be clear on one point: I can't predict the short-term movements of the stock market. I haven't the faintest idea as to whether stocks will be higher or lower a month—or a year—from now.

~ Warren Buffet

The advance is permanent; the declines are temporary.

~ Nick Murray

Guaranteed Minimum Death Benefit Rider – a rider added to annuity contracts which guarantees the amount that you have deposited in case of your death, regardless of market fluctuations. Your heir always receives at least what you deposited into the account originally, or a new amount set each year on the contract date if that amount is higher. This matters for the beneficiary or heir only, not the account holder. The account holder is guaranteed nothing while they are still living.

Example: Client deposits $500,000; account goes down to $420,000 due to market fluctuation. Client dies; beneficiary gets $500,000. There is sometimes a charge for the rider and sometimes not.

Guaranteed Income Benefit or *GIB* – a rider added to some variable annuities that will guarantee a certain percent of account value as a continuing periodic withdrawal into the future, regardless of account value. For example, a 5% annual rate of withdrawal based on the original deposit. If the original deposit was $500,000, then this could mean $25,000 withdrawal per year guaranteed, regardless of account fluctuation. If the account went to zero, the guarantee would require continued payment of the minimum withdrawal while the account holder was living.

The Whole Story

As an annuity is largely an investment vehicle—primarily aimed at deferring tax—you may be curious as to why you would see something, such as an IRA, invested in an annuity. While this is not common, it may be found. In some cases, it is an appropriate holding. This is precisely because of such features as the GIB listed above. Other mutual fund accounts not held in an annuity, regardless of how they are held, have no similar guarantee features attached to them in any way. Sometimes an investor who has had negative experiences in the past may wish to put their IRA into an annuity—not for the tax savings, as an IRA already does defer taxes—but for other features, such as this GIB, despite some additional fees attached to paying for it.

CHAPTER NINETEEN

Ways to Save Tax — Annuities Cost

The great advisors deal not in prediction and "performance" but in planning, perspective, and behavioral coaching.

~ Nick Murray

To enjoy a reasonable chance for continued better-than-average results, the investor must follow policies which are (1) inherently sound and promising, and (2) are not popular in Wall Street.

~ Benjamin Graham

Mortality and Expense, M & E – refers to certain charges which exist only on variable annuities, which covers, for example, the mortality guarantee, which means the company will pay out at least the original deposit and not less in the event of death.

Rider – an additional privilege or feature which *rides* on top of an already existing policy, usually of life insurance. An example could be a rider which pays a certain amount of insurance money if the person finds they are terminally ill. Or a rider on an annuity that guarantees a certain amount of withdrawal. Sometimes riders are free and sometimes there is a further charge for a rider. They allow customization to fit a particular account holder.

CHAPTER TWENTY

Protecting the Money and the Income —
Life Insurance

The reason why markets react only to data that differ from expectations is that the prices of securities in actively traded markets already include expected information.

~ Jeremy Siegel

Investment is most intelligent when it is most businesslike.

~ Benjamin Graham

Life Insurance – arrangement for a lump sum of money to be paid to a beneficiary after a person's death. The idea is to "indemnify (make up for) a loss." In other words, to make things the same financially as if the person was still around. It is not supposed to be a bonus or extra money, just an arrangement to keep things the same as if the one earning it were still present.

Term Life Insurance – a type of insurance which lasts for a specified term only. Its most common use is in insuring a parent during the time that children are not yet grown. The entire premium payment goes to pay for insurance cost only. There is nothing left that goes into any other account. It is therefore considerably cheaper than any type of "cash value" insurance such as ***Whole Life, Universal Life,*** or ***Variable Universal Life***. The problem is that it only lasts for a certain number of years, then the premium rises too high as you age, and you have to give up the insurance.

Premium – payment made on a life insurance policy, sometimes also loosely used to refer to the payment made into an annuity.

Death Benefit (also called ***Face Value*** or ***Face Amount***) – the full amount of money in life insurance that would be paid to a beneficiary if the insured dies.

Life insurance product features and availability vary by state. Restrictions and limitations may apply. For federal income tax purposes, life insurance death benefits generally pay income tax-free to beneficiaries pursuant to IRC Sec. 101(a)(1). In certain situations, however, life insurance death benefits may be partially or wholly taxable. Please consult a financial professional for additional information. All guarantees are based on the claims-paying ability of the insuring company.

CHAPTER TWENTY-ONE

Protecting the Money and the Income — Cash Value Life Insurance

In short, bad news is an investor's best friend. It lets you buy a slice of America's future at a marked-down price.

~ Warren Buffet

The market is fond of making mountains out of molehills and exaggerating ordinary vicissitudes into major setbacks. Even a mere lack of interest or enthusiasm may impel a price decline to absurdly low levels.

~ Benjamin Graham

Cash Value Insurance, also ***Permanent Insurance*** – a way of referring to either whole life insurance, universal life insurance, or variable universal life insurance.

Whole Life Insurance – this was the original insurance which was the first to last for the "whole life" as opposed to only a certain number of years. It does this by charging the person extra at the beginning and putting the extra amount in a sort of "savings account" which grows over time and then helps to pay for the greater premiums towards the end of a person's life so that the policy does not expire or need to be canceled, as in term insurance. It is useful currently to those who want the most complete guarantees regardless of cost.

Universal Life Insurance – Life insurance in which extra amount of premium payments not going directly towards the cost of life insurance are invested in an interest-bearing account, typically earning less than what would be earned long term in a Variable Universal Life policy and a bit more than a Whole Life policy. Universal Life is also more flexible than Whole Life for the insured. They may usually skip payments, pay more or less premium at times, lower the face amount, and so on, without penalty.

Variable Universal Life (VUL) – This means life insurance in which extra amount of premium payments not going directly towards the cost of insurance go into mutual funds as opposed to a fixed investment earning interest only, such as either Universal Life or Whole Life. It was developed in answer to those who complained that they could do a better job themselves of investing the money that was set aside for them in a Whole Life policy.

Survivor Life Insurance, or ***Second to Die*** – is a type of life insurance where both spouses are insured at the same time, and the death benefit is paid only on the second to die. This can be in some cases useful for paying estate or income taxes due by family members after the husband and wife have both died.

Chapter Fifteen through Twenty-One

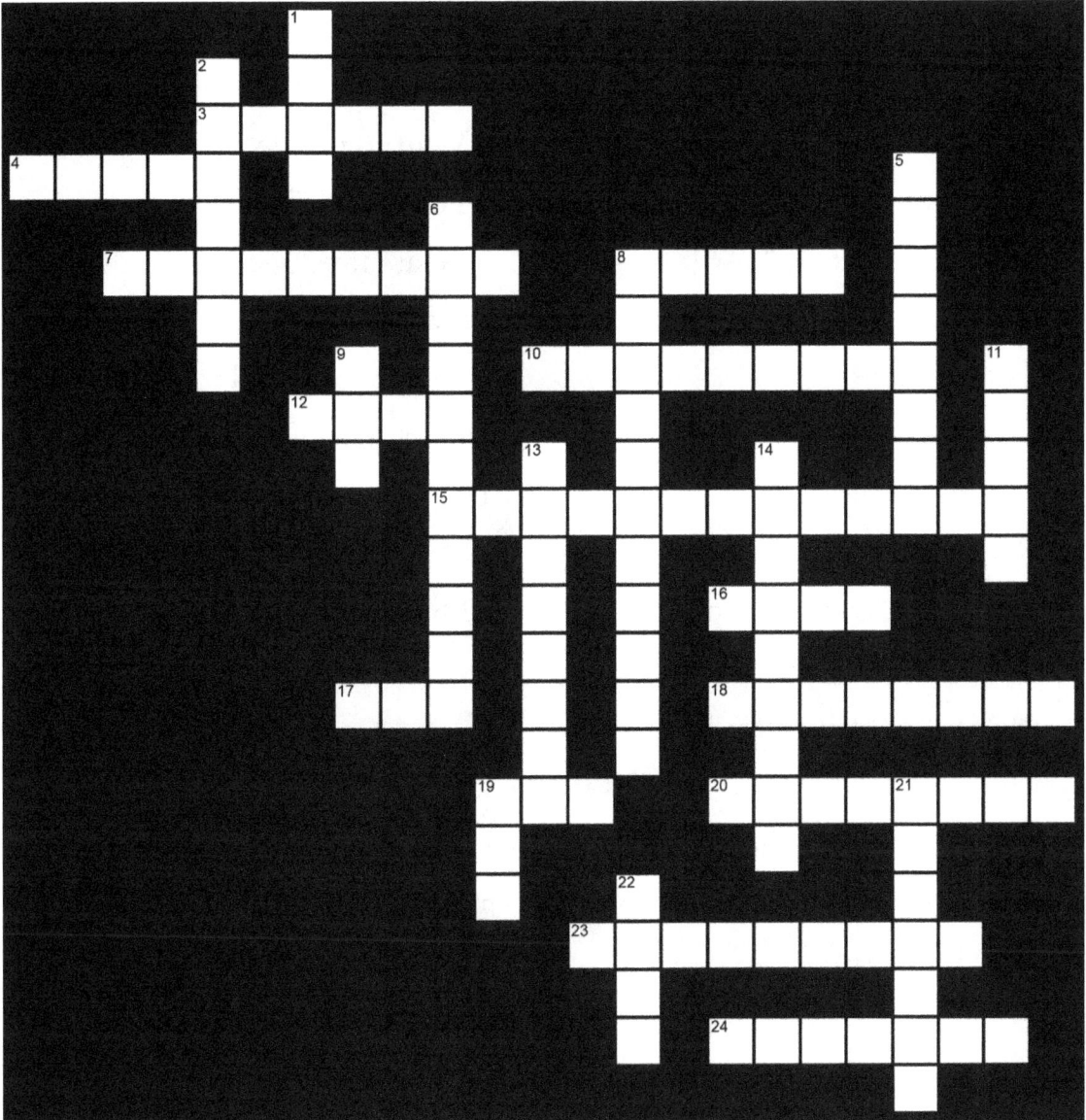

Across

3 Customization

4 Original insurance

7 Flexible insurance

8 Guaranteed no loss

10 For profit companies

12 Indemnify loss

15 Similar to fixed annuity

16 Taxed first

17 Premium to mutual funds

18 Limited term

19 Rerement plans acronym

20 Invested in mutual funds

23 Same as permanent

24 No control by investor

Down

1 Guaranteed deposit

2 Payment

5 When a stock is sold

6 Wait to pay tax

8 For nonprofits

9 Guaranteed income

11 Variable annuity expense

13 Same as second to die

14 On personal income

19 For anyone's retirement

21 Unlimited tax deferral

22 Same as death benefit

WORD LIST

ANNUITY	FUNDTAX	MANDE	TERMLIFE
CASHVALUE	GIB	PREMIUM	UNIVERSAL
EQUITYINDEXED	GMDB	RIDERS	VARIABLE
FACE	INCOMETAX	ROTH	VUL
FIXED	IRA	STOCKTAX	WHOLE
FOUROONEK	IRC	SURVIVOR	
FOUROTHREEB	LIFE	TAXDEFERRAL	

CHAPTER TWENTY-TWO

Protecting the Money and the Income — Life Insurance Guarantees

With the abundance of financial news, information, and commentary at our beck and call, it is extraordinarily difficult to stay aloof from market opinion. As a result, one's impulse is to capitulate to fear when the market is plunging or to greed when stocks are soaring.

~ Jeremy Siegel

The speculative public is incorrigible. In financial terms, it cannot count beyond 3. It will buy anything, at any price, if there seems to be some "action" in progress. It will fall for any company identified with "franchising," computers, electronics, science, technology, or what have you, when the particular fashion is raging.

~ Benjamin Graham

Lapse – said of a life insurance policy – to cease coverage, usually due to lack of premium payments.

No Lapse – a provision in a life insurance policy which prevents the policy from lapsing as long as agreed payments are made according to schedule, regardless of what happens to the cash values, depending upon interest rates or market investments.

Accumulation Value – a term that refers to the full cash value in a life insurance policy, as compared with the cash surrender value.

Cash Surrender Value – the amount of money that you can withdraw from your annuity or life insurance policy if you asked for all the money right now.

CHAPTER TWENTY-THREE

Switching the Money
from One Place to Another

An investor will succeed by coupling good business judgment with an ability to insulate his thoughts and behavior from the super-contagious emotions that swirl about the marketplace.
~ Warren Buffet

The investor can scarcely take seriously the innumerable predictions which appear almost daily and are his for the asking.
~ Benjamin Graham

Transfer of Funds – this is the usual description of transfer when funds are going from one investment to the same type of investment. For example, moving funds from one 403(b) plan to another 403(b) plan is called a *transfer*.

Rollover of Funds – when the funds are going from one type of investment to a different type of investment, this is called a *rollover*, not a transfer. For example, moving funds from a 401(k) to an IRA would be considered a rollover.

The Whole Story

Many people loosely use the word *rollover* to describe any transfer of funds. While not technically correct, it is important to be aware of this to avoid confusion.

1035 Exchange – this refers to a transfer according to IRS Code number 1035. (There are obviously over 1000 IRS Code sections.) This applies to an annuity exchange. Since an annuity usually has some gains that have not been taxed, the question arises when an annuity is transferred from one company to another: Are the gains then taxed? This IRS Code covers this question and says that as long as it is done with a 1035 exchange, that such taxes would not be payable and would continue to be deferred at the new company. As part of this transaction, one company sends records to the other of exactly how much is taxable.

CHAPTER TWENTY-FOUR

Taking Money Out

*I don't like to opine on the stock market, and again I emphasize that I
have no idea what the market will do in the short term.*
~ Warren Buffet

*So, don't go thinking that, if you're 59 and planning to retire at 63,
you're within the five-years-no-stocks window. That rule only applies
when you'll need your principal within 5 years. A retiree won't.*
~ Nick Murray

Required Minimum Distribution, RMD – refers to the minimum distributions (withdrawals) which are required by the IRS from a tax-sheltered plan or IRA when the person reaches seventy-three years old. They must take out a small percentage each year starting at this age. There is usually a 10% penalty for taking out money too soon, before age fifty-nine-and-a-half, but an up to 25% penalty for failing to take it out when required, after age seventy-three.

Pension – fixed sum paid regularly to a person retired from service. Usually, the pension continues for life.

Distribution, Withdrawal – taking out funds from a retirement account is usually referred to as a *distribution*. Such withdrawal may likely be subject to tax, similar to receiving a paycheck.

Always be sure to reference IRS.gov for current tax laws, as they are subject to change.

CHAPTER TWENTY-FIVE

Taking Money Out — Annuities

It has been my observation that it is so difficult to time correctly the near-term price movements of an attractive stock that the profits made in the few instances when this stock is sold and subsequently replaced at significantly lower prices are dwarfed by the profits lost when timing is wrong.

~ Philip Fisher

A simple rule dictates my buying: Be fearful when others are greedy, and be greedy when others are fearful.

~ Warren Buffet

Annuitize – refers to a special arrangement where money is taken out of an annuity a little at a time in equal payments until it is all gone. Once the arrangement is set up, it can never be changed. It is usually extremely unpopular for this reason.

The Whole Story

It may be ironic that one of the original purposes of an annuity, to guarantee income for life, was for a long time used minimally. Such guarantee of life income has returned to more frequent use as an optional rider on many annuities for an additional fee which allows for a guarantee of a minimum income but does not lock up the rest of the funds irrevocably as in annuitization.

Automatic Withdrawal – a method of taking funds out of an annuity account on a periodic basis. The opposite of putting them in on a periodic basis. Also, the opposite of *annuitizing*. You set up the periodic withdrawals but have flexibility: you can raise or lower or cancel the withdrawals whenever you like, unlike annuitization.

Surrender Penalty – the amount that someone would lose if they took all their money out of an annuity or life insurance policy in one lump sum.

Free Withdrawal – annuities that have surrender penalties frequently have a free withdrawal feature that allows withdrawal of something like 10% per year without penalty.

The Whole Story

Regarding surrender penalties, it is important for any investor to be fully aware of surrender penalties on annuities and how this may affect their ability to be in control of their funds, transfer them to another product of their choice, and be free from restrictions.

CHAPTER TWENTY-SIX

Transferring Money at Death — Methods

If the market falls, reporters pick a reason from the bearish pile; if the market rises, they pick a reason from the bullish set.

~ Jeremy Siegel

Thus, the investor who permits himself to be stampeded or unduly worried by unjustified market declines in his holdings is perversely transforming his basic advantage into a basic disadvantage. That man would be better off if his stocks had no market quotation at all, for he would then be spared the mental anguish caused him by other persons' mistakes of judgment.

~ Benjamin Graham

Contract – one method of transferring funds at death is by contract. This occurs in the case of insurance products, such as life insurance and annuities. A beneficiary is listed on the contract and at death all funds are transferred or paid to the beneficiary. Such listing is not affected by a will or trust. Another transfer by contract is real estate, where title to a property is listed as joint tenants, for example. In this case, the joint owner immediately takes possession of the entire property at death of the other owner. Again, this is not affected by will or trust.

Will – assets which are not in any way controlled by contract may transfer by will. A will is a simple way to leave a small amount of assets to heirs. For affluent individuals and families, usually a will only is inadequate.

Trust – this refers to an arrangement which includes some trust from one party to another but in an official sort of capacity. The person setting up the trust is called the *trustor* (the person doing the trusting). The person who watches over the trust is called the *trustee* (the person who is trusted) and the person who eventually receives what is in the trust is called the *beneficiary*.

> Example: You want to leave some money to your child but want them to have it only after age twenty-five. You set up a trust. When you die, the trust is presided over by a trustee who can be trusted to wait until your child is twenty-five to give them the money. A trust has certain tax advantages compared to a will. A trust can extend through time. Also, a trust is free of probate fees.

Gift – assets may be transferred by gift. In the cases of smaller estates, there is generally no advantage to transferring assets by gift before death.

CHAPTER TWENTY-SEVEN

Transferring Money at Death — to Whom?

You don't try and buy businesses worth $83 million for $80 million. You leave yourself an enormous margin. When you build a bridge, you insist it can carry 30,000 pounds, but you only drive 10,000 pound trucks across it. And that same principle works in investing.
~ Warren Buffet

The lesson is that markets and the economy are often out of sync.
~ Jeremy Siegel

Beneficiary – is a person or heir to whom assets will be transferred upon death.

Primary Beneficiary - the immediate beneficiary listed.

Contingent Beneficiary - refers to a beneficiary who is the one who will inherit the account if the first (primary) beneficiary is already deceased. In most cases, once a death occurs, the funds will pass on to the primary beneficiary. The naming of a contingent beneficiary only comes into play if there is a death of the primary beneficiary before the holder of the account has a chance to change the beneficiary due to the death of the primary beneficiary. This would be likely only when such death of account holder and primary beneficiary occurred relatively close together in time.

CHAPTER TWENTY-EIGHT

Transferring Money at Death — Taxes and Fees

It is very discomforting for many to learn that most movements in the market are random and do not have any identifiable cause or reason.
~ Jeremy Siegel

In current mathematical approaches to investment decisions, it has become standard practice to define "risk" in terms of average price variations or "volatility". . . . We find this use of the word "risk" more harmful than useful for sound investment decisions–because it places too much emphasis on market fluctuations.
~ Benjamin Graham

Estate Taxes – these are taxes *completely separate from income taxes*. Estate taxes are assessed only at death on property that passes on to inheritors and usually only if the amount is pretty large, in the millions of dollars. The amount of the tax can be as much as 50%.

Unlimited Marital Exemption – a spouse may transfer unlimited amounts to the other upon death with no assessment of any estate tax.

Probate – the process that an estate goes through after someone's death in which their assets are sorted out among heirs. Probate goes through the state and has various fees and other costs and is completely public, which some people don't like. Having a trust is private, and also saves the probate fees.

Word Origin
Probate **comes from the Latin "to prove."**

CHAPTER TWENTY-NINE

Transferring Money at Death — Saving Taxes and Fees

When the price of a stock can be influenced by a "herd" on Wall Street
with prices set at the margin by the most emotional person,
or the greediest person, or the most depressed person,
it is hard to argue that the market always prices rationally.
In fact, market prices are frequently nonsensical.

~ Warren Buffet

In the event of hyper-inflation, stocks will be, by far,
the best performing financial assets.

~ Jeremy Siegel

Stepped Up Basis at Death – means that assets or accounts have an original *basis*. This is usually the amount for which the account or asset was purchased. Over time, this amount usually increases, and while the owner is living, would be taxable if they sold the asset or withdrew the funds. According to current IRS law, if the owner dies, there is then a *step up* of basis, meaning that the basis moved up to the new value at the time of death. In many cases, this may save large amounts of taxes on increased value of the asset before death.

The Whole Story

While the stepped up basis at death may save significant amounts of tax on a real estate property passing from parent to child, or similar taxes on tax deferred accounts, planning for such savings can be tricky at best. You probably do not know how long you will live. There can be good reasons to sell assets, particularly market-invested accounts, at the time you wish, not waiting till death, when they may have gone up, but also in some cases could have gone down. Therefore, while stepped up basis at death is a good rule to be aware of, it is by no means the primary tool in planning for tax savings on passing assets to heirs.

Chapters Twenty-two through Twenty-nine

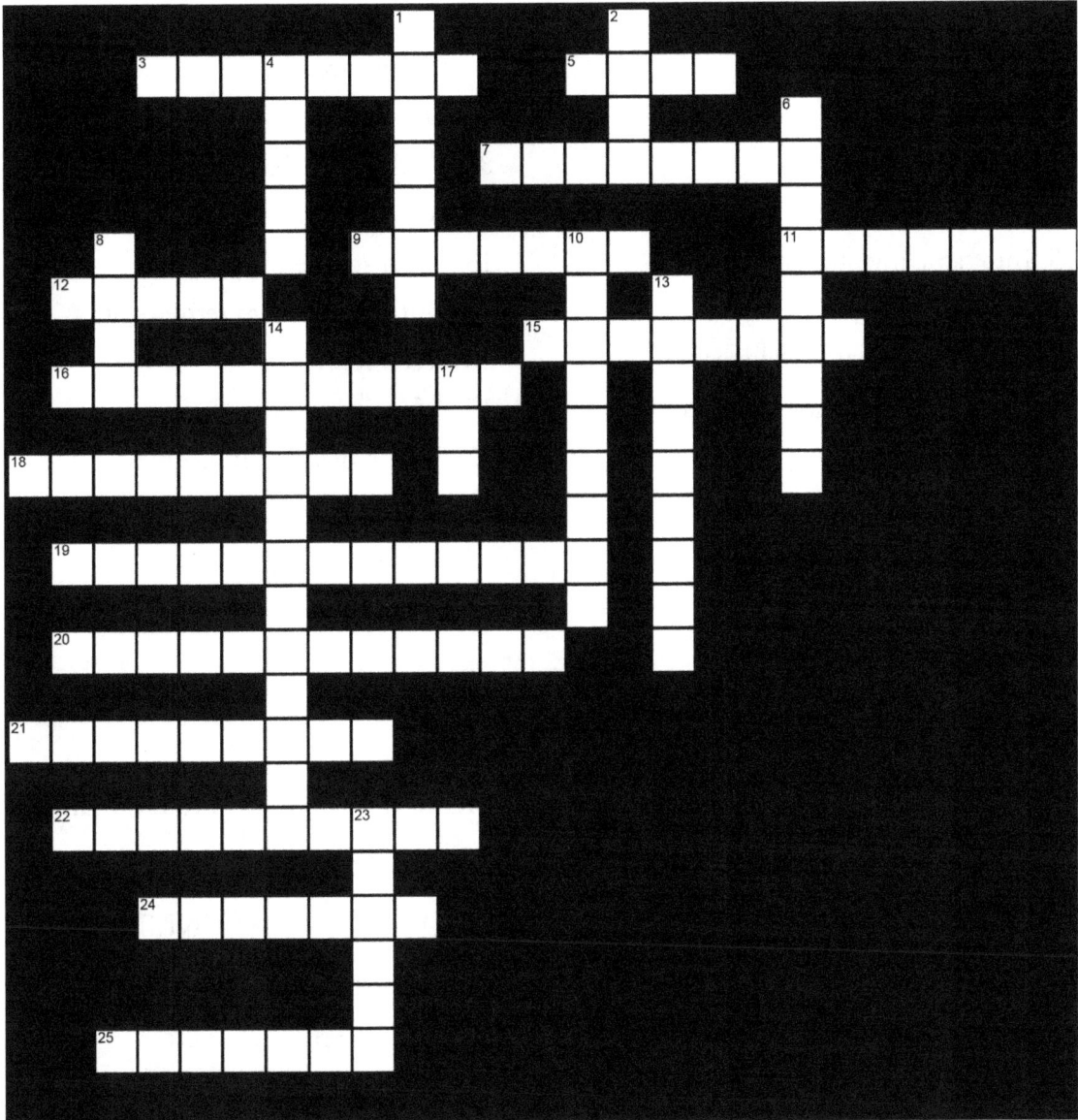

Across

3 To another type investment

5 Leave to heirs simply

7 Transfer at death

9 Policy provision

11 Immediate heir

12 Transfer with no probate

15 Into same investment

16 An heir

18 Withdrawal that is changeable

19 Exchange nontaxable transfer

20 Full cash value

21 Unchanging withdrawal

22 Primary dies first

24 Surrender

25 Estate transfer if no trust

Down

1 Fixed sum for life

2 Transfer assets while alive

4 Cease coverage

6 Over amount of purchase

8 Withdrawal 10 percent

10 Available now

13 From spouse to spouse

14 Withdrawal from retirement account

17 After age seventy-three

23 Tax on death, not income

WORD LIST

ACCUMULATION	ESTATE	PRIMARY	TRANSFER
ANNUITIZE	FREE	PROBATE	TRUST
AUTOMATIC	GIFT	RMD	UNLIMITED
BENEFICIARY	LAPSE	ROLLOVER	WILL
CONTINGENT	NOLAPSE	STEPPEDUP	
CONTRACT	PENALTY	SURRENDER	
DISTRIBUTION	PENSION	TENTHIRTYFIVE	

Conclusion

I hope the preceding pages and exercises are educational.

It is now time to evaluate what you have learned in terms of your own investments.

List Accounts by Overall Classification

The first step is to list exactly what investments you have. There may be more to this than you think. Rather than say, "I have three accounts and two life insurance policies," it is better to list each account and then name exactly what type of account it is.

For example, if the account is an *IRA*, is it a *Traditional IRA* or a *Roth IRA?* If you have *life insurance*, is it *Term Life Insurance* or is it *Permanent Cash Value Insurance?*

First, list all your accounts with the *overall classification* noted. If you have trouble on this step, refer to the terminology definitions to assist you. You might list something like the following if for a family:

A. 401(k) retirement account for spouse A
B. Spouse A IRA
C. Spouse B IRA
D. Term life insurance on Spouse A
E. Term life insurance on spouse B

List by How Invested

The next step is to determine how the account is invested. For example, an IRA could be invested in:

- Mutual funds with an individual fund company
- Mutual funds in a brokerage account
- Individual stocks
- A bank account
- A certificate of deposit

So, you may list:

A. 401(k) with Fidelity
B. Spouse A IRA in brokerage account
C. Spouse B IRA with American Funds

List Specific Investments

Determine in which you are invested by carefully examining the statement for that account. Again, if it is not clear, review the terminology definitions until you know in which you are invested.

Next, note or list the names of the individual investments. An example could be:

- A mutual fund
- B mutual fund
- C mutual fund
- Money market

Congratulations! You have now listed your accounts and divided them into types of investment. While these steps may seem simple, you have likely now surpassed the understanding of the average investor and have an idea of what accounts you are holding, their tax status, and category.

Steps from this point may or may not be easy without the assistance of an advisor who has access to your information and familiarity with how to find further specifics on investments.

List Allocations

The next step is to determine how your investments are allocated. To do this, first review Chapter Nine: Making Money Grow — Mutual Fund Types.

Then divide the investments of each account by allocation type. For example, in IRA:

- A mutual fund - large growth
- B mutual fund - large growth
- C mutual fund - mid growth
- Money market

To accomplish this step, you may first simply look at the name of the funds. Sometimes they clearly say "large growth" as part of the name. Unfortunately, many times they will not. If so, you may look for them online, or turn to a qualified financial advisor to assist.

Review and Determine a Course of Action

In many cases, the allocations will turn out to be something like the above, overweighted in one or two categories and leaving out others altogether. Such may create less long-term safety.

Review Return

At this point, review Chapter Fourteen: *How Did It Do?* and all terminology in that section. The returns of each category would now be compared to average returns as represented by an index of that particular category. Again, this may not be possible without the assistance of an advisor who has access to and familiarity with how to find further specifics on investments and the appropriate programs which provide this data.

SUMMARY

In a nutshell, the above steps give you a sequence that allows a basic evaluation of an investment portfolio. If these steps seem oversimplified, then you may already be someone who has advanced understanding of financial areas. In the Introduction, we said, "The definitions are not meant for financial advisors, financial professionals, professors, economists, or anyone with advanced understanding of financial areas." So again, if you are other than the above, I sincerely hope that you have benefited from these pages and may be able to put them to use.

Now you are a master, or at least more proficient, in the basic terminology which is the foundation of investments and retirement planning. Congratulations again on your progress and best wishes for success with your newfound knowledge.

Next Steps

Review the book and do the crosswords again, until proficient.

Go to my website, enoughmoneytoliveon.com for contact information.

Send me an email to request a consultation: bob.kaye@securitiesamerica.com.

Send an email with any comments or suggestions or requests for the next revision of this book.

References

Buffet, Warren. "Buy American. I Am." *New York Times*. Op Ed, 2008.

Buffet, Warren. Preface from Benjamin Graham's *The Intelligent Investor*. Harper & Row, 1973.

Cunningham, Lawrence. *The Essays of Warren Buffet*. Lawrence Cunningham, 2015.

Fisher, Philip A. *Common Stocks and Uncommon Profits*. John Wiley & Sons, 2003 (first edition, Harper & Brothers, 1958).

Graham, Benjamin. *The Intelligent Investor,* Harper & Row, 1973.

Graham, Benjamin, and David Dodd. *Security Analysis*. The McGraw Hill Companies, 1934.

Murray, Nick. *Simple Wealth, Inevitable Wealth*. The Nick Murray Company, 2013.

Siegel, Jeremy. *Stocks for the Long Run*. McGraw-Hill, 1998.

Crossword Puzzle Answer Key

Chapters One through Six

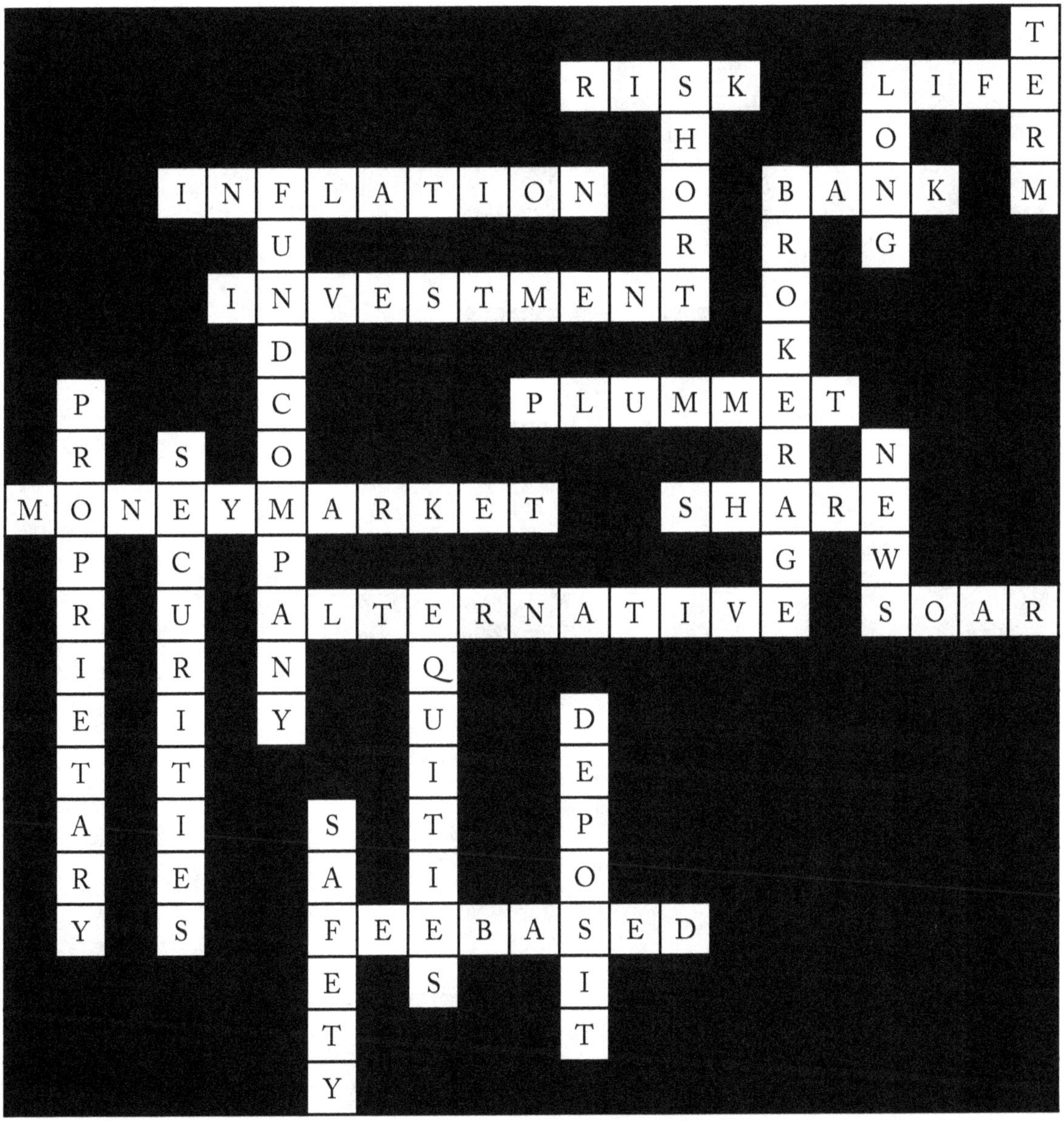
TERM
RISK
LIFE
SHORT
LONG
INFLATION
BANK
FUND
INVESTMENT
BROKERAGE
PLUMMET
PROPRIETARY
SECURITIES
COMPANY
MONEYMARKET
SHARE
NEW
ALTERNATIVE
SOAR
EQUITIES
DEPOSIT
SAFETY
FEEBASED

Chapters Seven through Eleven

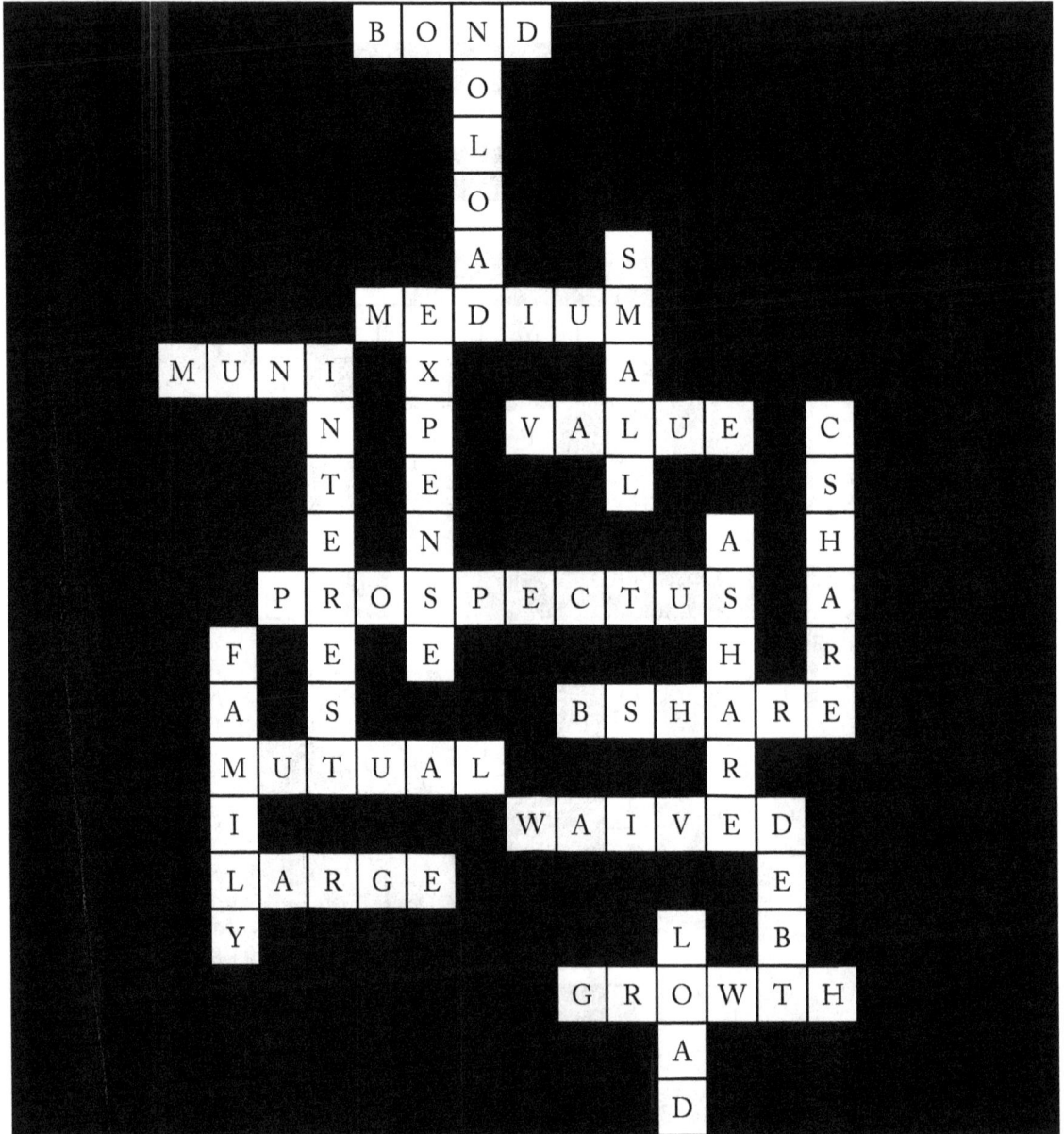

A completed crossword puzzle with the following filled-in answers:

- BOND
- NOLOAD
- MEDIUM
- SMALL
- MUNI
- EXPENSE
- VALUE
- INTEREST
- PROSPECTUS
- FEES
- FAMILY
- MUTUAL
- BSHARE
- CSHARE
- SHAREHOLDER
- WAIVED
- LARGE
- GROWTH
- LOAD

Chapters Twelve through Fourteen

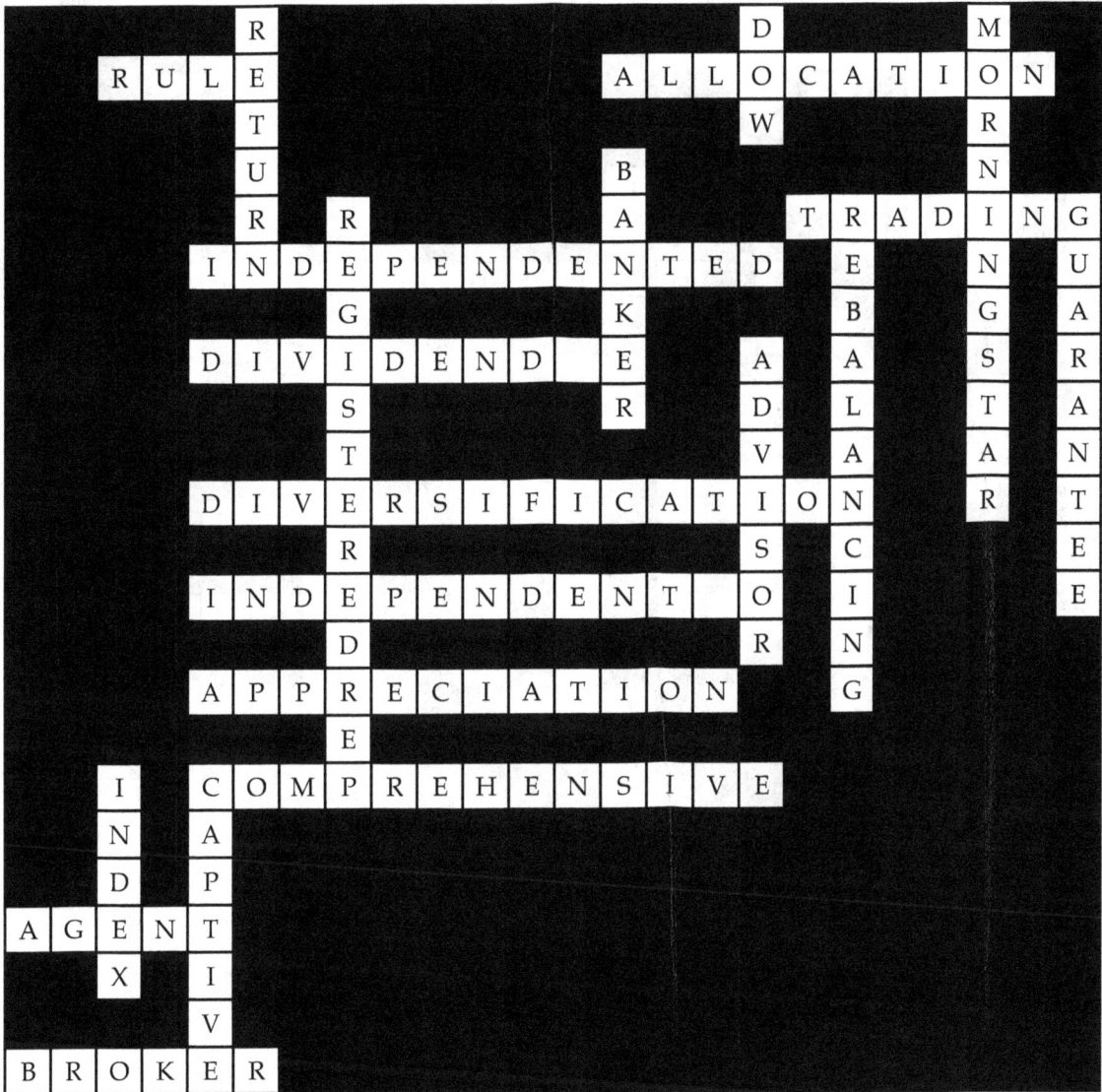

```
                R                         D               M
      R  U  L  E           A  L  L  O  C  A  T  I  O  N
                T                         W               R
                U                  B                      N
                R        R         A      T  R  A  D  I  N  G
         I  N  D  E  P  E  N  D  E  N  T  E  D         N     U
                G         K            E     B         S     A
      D  I  V  I  D  E  N  D     E     A     A         T     R
                S         K     R     D     L         A     A
                T               A     V     A         R     N
      D  I  V  E  R  S  I  F  I  C  A  T  I  O  N         T     T
                R               S     N     C               E
      I  N  D  E  P  E  N  D  E  N  T     O     I               E
                D               R     C           N
      A  P  P  R  E  C  I  A  T  I  O  N     G
                E
         I     C  O  M  P  R  E  H  E  N  S  I  V  E
         N     A
         D     P
   A  G  E  N  T  I
         X     I
               V
   B  R  O  K  E  R
```

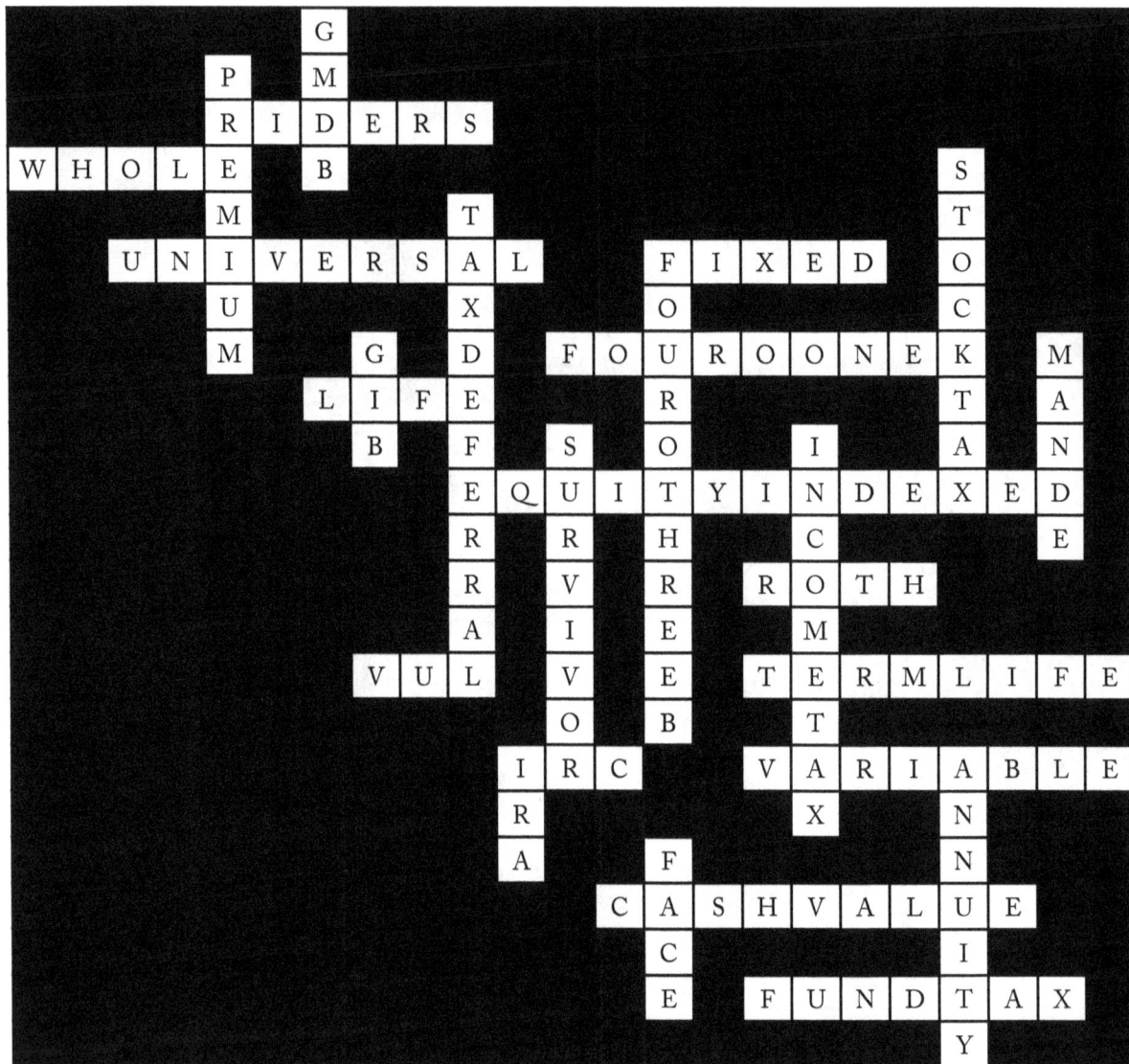

A crossword puzzle grid containing the following answers:

- WHOLE
- RIDERS
- PREMIUM
- UNIVERSAL
- GMIB
- GMDB
- TAXDEFERRAL
- LIFE
- FIXED
- STOCKTANDMANE
- FOUROONEK
- FOURONETHREEB
- SURVIVORSHIP
- EQUITYINDEXED
- ROTH
- ICOMMT
- VUL
- TERMLIFE
- IRC
- IRA
- VARIABLE
- TAX
- FACE
- CASHVALUE
- FUNDTAX
- ANNUITY

Chapters Twenty-two through Twenty-nine

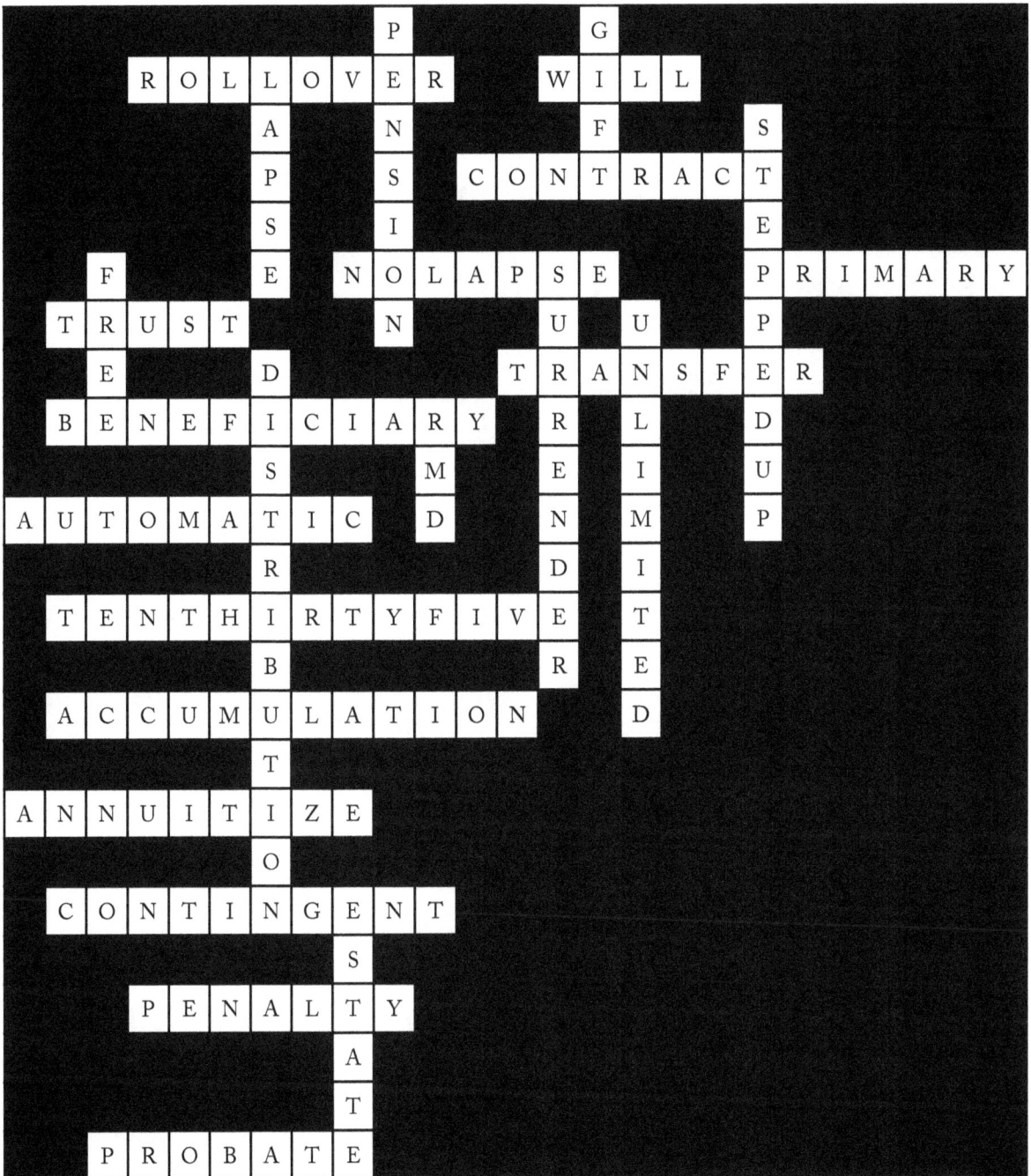

ROLLOVER

WILL

CONTRACT

NOLAPSE

PRIMARY

TRUST

TRANSFER

BENEFICIARY

AUTOMATIC

TENTHIRTYFIVE

ACCUMULATION

ANNUITIZE

CONTINGENT

PENALTY

PROBATE

About the Author

Bob Kaye is a Personal Wealth Manager who specializes in working with professionals in relation to their retirement benefit plans. He helps individuals and their families transition into retirement and guides them toward achieving financial security. He does this by working with their own advisors as well as his own team of experts. He limits his clientele to a number of clients for whom he feels he can provide the most value. He is glad to get together for an initial meeting to determine whether he may be able to accept and work with a new client in the future.

He has been acting as Financial Advisor for professionals for twenty-five years. He is a Registered Representative with Securities America, Inc, Member FINRA/SIPC. He is a fully licensed investment advisor representative in insurance, annuities, mutual funds, stocks and bonds and is also qualified as a Certified Funds Specialist®, a designation held by only about 1% of those licensed to work with mutual funds.[12] The CFS is the oldest designation in the mutual fund industry, coming into existence in 1988. He is certified additionally

---

12 The Institute of Business and Finance

as a Chartered Life Underwriter®, the landmark designation of the American College. The CLU® is respected internationally as risk management's highest standard of knowledge and trust. Since 1927, the American College has awarded this designation to professionals who obtain the advanced education to address the insurance needs of every client they serve.

His experience also includes tax return preparation, real estate purchase, and refinance. He is a member of The Premier Association of Financial Professionals® and the Association of Independent Financial Advisors. He currently spends a majority of his time in the Southern California area working directly with clients.

Retirement Planning Associates, headed by Bob Kaye, offers complete wealth management services including investment consulting with appropriate tax strategies that best take advantage of available resources using fitting investment vehicles. Wealth management further includes advanced planning that breaks down into wealth enhancement: return and safety with investment; wealth transfer: estate planning and generational transfer at death; wealth protection: appropriate life insurance covering all aspects; and charitable giving tailored to desires of clients with tax-advantaged priorities. Retirement Planning Associates is affiliated with Securities America, Inc., one of the nation's largest and most successful independent general broker/dealers.

Recognitions and Awards:

Past California State Chairman of the Membership Communications Committee for the Premier Association of Financial Professionals®

Awarded Lifetime Membership and Honor Roll in the Premier Association of Financial Professionals®

He has been pleased to be the recipient of the President's Volunteer Service Award in a Capitol Hill ceremony in Washington, D.C., for his volunteer activities concerning human rights.

The P resident's C ouncil o n S ervice a nd C ivic P articipation l aunched t he President's Volunteer Service Award in 2003. The award (PVSA) is the premier volunteer awards program, encouraging citizens to live a life of service through presidential gratitude and national recognition.

He is twice recipient of the Premier Association of Financial Professionals®, Financial Professionals Changing Lives Worldwide™ Quality of Life Grant Award in honor of his volunteerism.

He is recipient of the Sherman Oaks Chamber of Commerce Recognition Award for ten years of Chamber Membership in service to the community with recognition by US Congress, California State Assembly and Senate, County of Los Angeles, and City of Los Angeles.

When not involved as a Financial Advisor or volunteering with Human Rights, he can be found with his family in the summer sailing off the California coast or enjoying countrywide ski slopes in the winter.

Please visit his website, enoughmoneytoliveon.com, to find out more about working with Bob and for full disclosure.

www.ingramcontent.com/pod-product-compliance
Lightning Source LLC
Chambersburg PA
CBHW051413200326
41520CB00023B/7219